## 25 CYCLE ROUTES

# THE KINGDOM OF FIFE

### Erl B. Wilkie

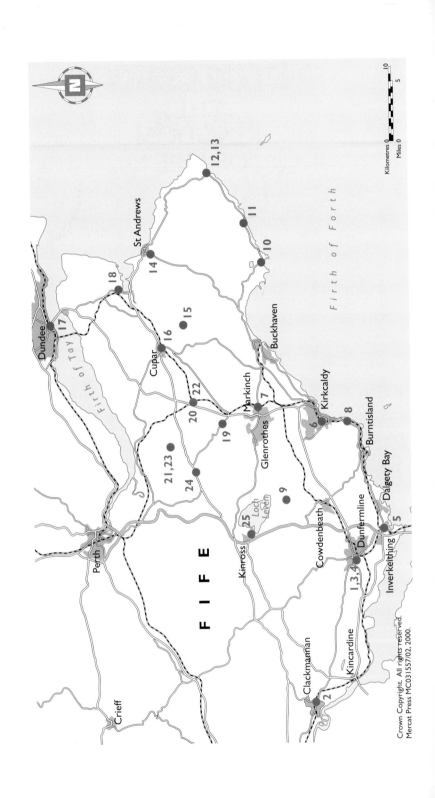

St Andrews

Dundee

Firth of Tay

Cupar

18

17

14

15

16

12,13

11

10

Buckhaven

Markinch

Kirkcaldy

20

22

7

19

Glenrothes

6

8

Burntisland

21,23

24

9

Firth of Forth

Perth

25

Loch Leven

Cowdenbeath

Dalgety Bay

F I F E

Kinross

Dunfermline

5

Crieff

Clackmannan

Inverkeithing

Kincardine

1,3,4

2

Kilometres 0          10

Miles 0          5

# 25 CYCLE ROUTES

# THE KINGDOM OF FIFE

### Erl B. Wilkie

With a Foreword by CTC

**KINGDOM OF FIFE**
Millennium Cycleways

A MILLENNIUM PROJECT
SUPPORTED BY FUNDS
FROM THE NATIONAL LOTTERY

Scottish Enterprise
Fife

KINGDOM OF
FIFE
TOURIST BOARD

# MERCAT PRESS

First published in 2000 by Mercat Press
at James Thin, 53 South Bridge
Edinburgh EH1 1YS
*www.mercatpress.com*

© Mercat Press 2000

ISBN: 1 84183 016 X

Also available in this series:
*25 Cycle Routes—Edinburgh and Lothian*
*25 Cycle Routes—In and Around Glasgow*
*25 Cycle Routes—Stirling and the Trossachs*

## Acknowledgements

The author wishes to thank Fife Council, Scottish Enterprise Fife and
the Kingdom of Fife Tourist Board for the financial support given for the
publication of this book. A particular thank you must go to Sharon Rice-
Jones of The Kingdom of Fife Millennium Cycle Ways Project for her
support and help and to Graeme Pate, a good friend, who helped me
with the index.

The publisher acknowledges with thanks the financial support of Fife
Council, Scottish Enterprise Fife and the Kingdom of Fife Tourist Board.
The major funding for the Fife Millennium Cycle Ways Project comes
from the Millennium Commission, and so the Commission is gratefully
acknowledged here also. Finally, the publisher's thanks are due to the
author who supplied all of the pictures used.

# CONTENTS

Foreword by CTC ................................................................ vi

Introduction ..................................................................... viii

Route 1 — Dunfermline to Culross ................................... 1

Route 2 — Clackmannan to Culross .................................. 7

Route 3 — Dunfermline to Charlestown ............................ 11

Route 4 — Dunfermline to Kelty ...................................... 15

Route 5 — Inverkeithing to Crossgates via Aberdour .......... 19

Route 6 — Kirkcaldy to Auchtertool ................................ 25

Route 7 — Markinch to Kennoway .................................. 29

Route 8 — Kinghorn to Lochgelly .................................... 33

Route 9 — Kelty to Ballingry ........................................... 39

Route 10 — Elie and Earlsferry to Colinsburgh .................. 43

Route 11 — St Monance to Pittenweem ............................ 47

Route 12 — Crail to Anstruther ....................................... 51

Route 13 — Crail to Fife Ness ......................................... 55

Route 14 — St Andrews to Ceres ..................................... 59

Route 15 — Ceres to Lower Largo ................................... 63

Route 16 — Cupar to Bottomcraig via The Gauldry ........... 67

Route 17 — Dundee to Leuchars ..................................... 71

Route 18 — Leuchars to Tayport ..................................... 75

Route 19 — Falkland to Freuchie ..................................... 79

Route 20 — Freuchie to Ladybank ................................... 83

Route 21 — Auchtermuchty to Ladybank .......................... 87

Route 22 — Ladybank to Cupar via Cults Hill ................... 91

Route 23 — Auchtermuchty to Newburgh ......................... 97

Route 24 — Strathmiglo to Glenfarg ................................ 101

Route 25 — Kinross to Ballingry via Loch Leven ............... 105

Index ............................................................................. 108

# FOREWORD BY CTC

Cycling is healthy, environmentally-friendly—and above all fun! Travel at your own pace, meet people along the way and experience the real country. Explore parts of the country that you didn't know existed—and improve your fitness at the same time! Cycling is good for you, so go by bike, and you'll feel a whole lot better for it.

## Safety considerations and equipment needed

• Before you go cycling, check your bike thoroughly for broken, worn and/or loose parts. In particular, check for worn tyres and broken/loose spokes. Ensure that both brakes and the gear system are working well, with the chain lightly oiled and running smoothly. If in doubt your local bike shop will advise you further. Better to fix things now, than to spoil your ride later.

• Carry a cycle lock and key, and a small tool kit (spare inner tube, tyre levers, small adjustable spanner, puncture repair outfit, pump and Allen keys if your bike needs them).

• If you are really loading up for a big adventure your luggage should be on the bike not your back. A rear carrying rack is useful. Ideally pack everything into plastic bags inside a saddlebag or panniers properly secured to this rack. Check your load is balanced, and the weight doesn't affect the steering/handling of the bike. If you prefer to travel light you can fit most things into a bumbag.

• Always carry food and water/liquid. Cyclists are advised to drink little and often.

• Comfortable clothing is essential. For colder days wear two or three layers: you can take them off once you've warmed up and put them on if you cool off. Wet-weather gear is useful if you've

## METRIC MEASUREMENTS

At the beginning of each route, the distance is given in miles and kilometres. Within the text, all measurements are metric for simplicity (and indeed our Ordnance Survey maps are now all metric). However, it was felt that a conversion table might be useful to those readers who, like the author, still tend to think in miles.

The basic statistic to remember is that one kilometre is five-eighths of a mile. Half a mile is equivalent to 800 metres and a quarter-mile is 400 metres. Below that distance, yards and metres are little different in practical terms.

| km | miles |
| --- | --- |
| 1 | 0.625 |
| 1.6 | 1 |
| 2 | 1.25 |
| 3 | 1.875 |
| 3.2 | 2 |
| 4 | 2.5 |
| 4.8 | 3 |
| 5 | 3.125 |
| 6 | 3.75 |
| 6.4 | 4 |
| 7 | 4.375 |
| 8 | 5 |
| 9 | 5.625 |
| 10 | 6.25 |
| 16 | 10 |

got the space to carry it. For hot weather don't forget your sun cream and shades.

- You don't have to wear specialist cycle clothing to enjoy cycling. Padded shorts, gloves, cycling shoes, cycle helmets and much more can be purchased at cycle shops if you are interested. NB It is not compulsory to wear a helmet, and the choice is yours. CTC can provide further information on helmets if needed.

- Check your riding position is comfortable. Saddle height: when seated, place your heel on the pedal when it is at its lowest point. Your leg should be straight, and your knee just off the locked position. On the subject of riding comfort, many bikes are supplied with saddles designed for men (long and narrow). Women may prefer to sit on a saddle designed for women (shorter and wider at the back). These are available from bike shops.

- There is some useful information for cyclists in the *Highway Code*. This is available from garages, bookshops and may be found in your library.

- If you think that you may be cycling when it is dark, you will need to fit front and rear lights. (This is a legal requirement.) Lights and reflectors/reflective clothing are also useful in bad weather conditions.

- In the event of an accident, it is advisable to note the time and place of the incident, the names and addresses of those involved, details of their insurance company, and vehicle registration numbers and details of any witnesses. In the event of injury or damage, report the incident to the police immediately.

 **For further information about cycling...**

CTC (Cyclist's Touring Club) is Britain's largest cycling organisation, and can provide a wealth of information and advice about all aspects of cycling. CTC works on behalf of all cyclists to promote cycling and to protect cyclists' interests.

Membership includes free third-party insurance, legal aid, touring and technical information, a bi-monthly magazine and a cyclists' handbook.

For further details contact CTC at: Cotterell House, 69 Meadrow, Godalming, Surrey GU7 3HS; or telephone 01483 417217, fax 01483 426994; or e-mail *helpdesk@ctc.org.uk*; or visit the website: *www.ctc.org.uk*.

# INTRODUCTION

Fife Council has spent a great deal of time, effort and a substantial amount of money developing the Kingdom of Fife Millennium Cycle Ways, a network of signed cycle routes which span the entire Council area, setting cycling into the main framework of Fife's transport strategy. The Millennium Cycle Ways offer a unique opportunity to cycle throughout Fife in a relatively safe and pleasant manner. The main artery of the network is the circular Kingdom Route connecting the Forth Bridge with the Tay Bridge and back again, a distance of 168 km. There are also another 11 routes which circulate around and through the main arterial route. Finally there are local networks throughout many of the principal towns such as Dunfermline, Glenrothes and Kirkcaldy, making a total 500 km of signed cycle route available to cyclists of all ages and abilities. The western section of the Kingdom Route also forms part of the North Sea Cycle Route, a circular route from Norway through Scotland, England, Holland, Germany, Denmark, Sweden and back to Norway, and is some 5,932 km in length.

This book augments these routes by creating a total of 659 km of further routes throughout the length and breadth of Fife, meandering in, out and through the existing Kingdom of Fife Cycle Routes. The book illustrates the many and varied characteristics of the area: from its unique blend of industrial heritage and ancient history to its gently rolling hills and glens, its lochs, rivers, waterfalls and forests and its spectacularly beautiful coastline.

These routes vary in length from 8 km to 46 km and in difficulty from easy to very demanding.

For the most part the routes in this book use the network of minor roads which are so abundant in this part of the world. These have negligible vehicular traffic flows, and therefore are ideal for cycling. Many of the routes also connect with, and use lengths of, the existing Kingdom of Fife cycle network. There are only a very few difficult surfaces to negotiate along these routes and where these occur they are clearly indicated in the text. An easier alternative to these stretches of route has been offered in each case.

The off-road sections within these routes have been checked out carefully to ascertain the rights of access. However sometimes it is not clear if a stretch of path is, or is not, a right of way, since many in Scotland are informal. In such cases the responsibility lies with the individual who is cycling on the particular path or stretch of land. Remember that there is a law of trespass in Scotland, and although one cannot be prosecuted for crossing private land one can be sued for damage and one can be asked to leave by the shortest route. I would therefore offer the following guidelines:

1  If you come across a sign prohibiting you from a stretch of land, respect this and find an alternative route.

2  If you are about to enter private land knowingly, try, if feasible, to gain the owner's permission before doing so.

3  If, when you are cycling on a path or stretch of land, you are challenged, unless you are completely sure the land you are cycling on is public or is a right of way, then leave the area by the shortest available route.

4  When you are on any land, whether private or public, do not cause a nuisance in any way. Do not cause damage to crops, property, or fences. Close all gates and do not frighten farm animals.

5  Keep dogs under control at all times.

If these commonsense rules are applied then no one can have any justifiable grievance with you.

On occasion some of the routes use A and B class roads, but I have avoided using very busy roads except when they are an unavoidable short link between much quieter stretches of road. I feel that if these sections of road are used properly and with care they should not cause any problems and should not detract from the enjoyment of the overall route. However, the reader must make his or her own judgement about safety depending on the circumstances prevailing at the time. If in doubt do not attempt it!

Where possible the routes start and finish at railway stations. If, however, there is no railway in the vicinity of the route, it starts at a convenient car park.

I hope you will enjoy these routes which pass through very varied terrain and, I feel, show the Kingdom of Fife at its best.

Erl B. Wilkie

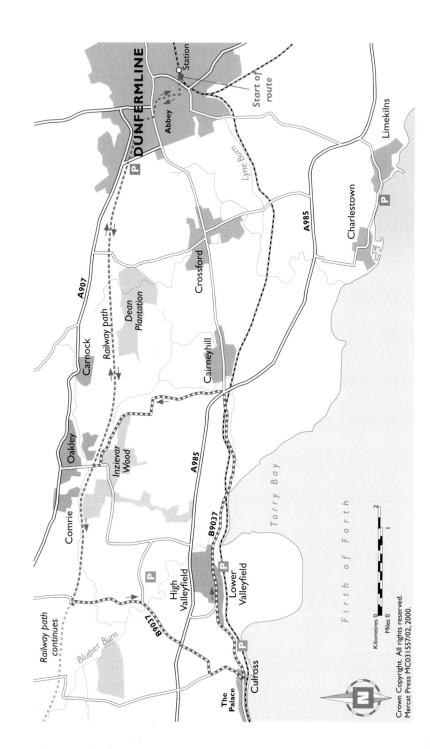

DUNFERMLINE

Station

Start of route

Abbey

Limekilns

Lyne Burn

A985

Charlestown

A907

Carnock

Railway path

Dean Plantation

Crossford

Cairneyhill

Oakley

Inzievar Wood

A985

Comrie

B9037

Torry Bay

High Valleyfield

Lower Valleyfield

Firth of Forth

Railway path continues

Bluther Burn

B9037

Culross

The Palace

Kilometres 0                    2
Miles 0        1

N

# DUNFERMLINE TO CULROSS

**D**unfermline became the royal capital of Scotland in 1058 when Malcolm Canmore succeeded King Lulach to the throne. Lulach, Macbeth's stepson, had only ruled for seven months before he was defeated in battle and killed by Malcolm Canmore at Lumphanan in 1057.

During Malcolm's reign, his wife Margaret, a devout Christian, brought the Celtic Church in Scotland into line with the Church of Rome. The existing church in Dunfermline was enlarged by her around 1070, and she brought Benedictine monks up from Canterbury to serve in it. Her youngest son, David I, established the Abbey here in 1130, and in 1329 King Robert I, the great Bruce, was buried here, joining nineteen other members of Scottish royal families. David's elder brother, Alexander I, granted a charter to the town in 1120 making it a Royal Burgh.

The Royal Palace was rebuilt by James IV in 1500 on the ruins of the earlier guest-house of the Abbey which had been burned down by Edward I in 1303.

## INFORMATION

**Distance:** 29 km (18.2 miles) circular route.

**Map:** OS Landranger, sheet 65; Kingdom of Fife Cycle Ways West Fife map.

**Start and finish:** Dunfermline Railway Station.

**Terrain:** For most of the way this route follows sections of the Kingdom of Fife Cycle Network. It is undulating with some short stretches of steeper gradients.

**Refreshments:** Available from many places in Dunfermline and Culross.

Dunfermline Palace.

It became favoured by the kings of Scotland and some were born there, the last being Charles I in 1600.

Along this route through Dunfermline there is a cluster of historic buildings, each having a significant role in the development of Scotland, so do take time to stop and look around. They include the birthplace, next to Pittencrieff Park, of Andrew Carnegie, the great Scots–American industrialist and philanthropist, who will always remain Dunfermline's number one son.

Andrew Carnegie's birthplace, Dunfermline.

Leave the station area and carry on through an underpass which links the station with Comley Park. Travel in a westerly direction to the junction with New Road and carry straight on into Priory Lane. After 200 m or so the road sweeps round to the left. Here carry straight on in a westerly direction, into a narrower street which is still Priory Lane. Turn right at the T-junction, where Andrew Carnegie's birthplace is situated, into St Margaret Street. Turn first left into Monastery Street, which becomes St Catherine's Wynd. Turn left into Bridge Street and carry straight on over the four-way junction into Chalmers Street. At the end of this street turn left into Golfdrum Street, which ends at William Street. Here turn right and carry on for 200 m to reach the access point to the cycleway. Turn left into an area set out as a car park, at the end of which the cycle path begins in a westerly direction.

As this route is clearly defined there is no need to describe it until East Grange some 9 km to the west, which is the last in a series of four industrial villages just to the north of the route. These are Carnock, Oakley, Comrie and Blairhall, and were all built to house workers in the coal and steel industries which once thrived in the area. Indeed, in the nineteenth century, Oakley was the proud possessor of six blast furnaces, which were part of the Oakley Iron Works.

On arriving at East Grange go through the gate to the right and along the path which leads to the B9037. Once here, turn left and follow this road under the cycleway above and on for 2 km to the A985. At the junction with this very busy road turn right and then immediately left on to the minor road signposted for Culross, and within 1 km this beautiful and historic village is reached. Today Culross is thought to be the finest example of a small seventeenth-century Scottish town.

Within its bounds, which have changed little in the last 300 years, there are many interesting buildings, some of which have been extensively restored by the National Trust for Scotland. These include the Palace, the Town House, the Study, Bessie Bar's Hall and the Abbey.

Culross was, according to folklore, founded by St Serf, and a story quoted in *Culross, A Companion to the Royal Burgh* (National Trust for Scotland) links the town and St Serf with the birth of Kentigern (St Mungo), the patron saint of Glasgow. In fact, nothing certain is known about St Serf and not much more is known about St Mungo apart from the date of his death, which, it seems, was c. 612. It is thought that he was probably born in the territory of the Gododdin on the northern shores of the Forth, and, of course, this would include Culross. Therefore, the story quoted about his birth could well be true—who knows?

The land around Culross Abbey was gifted to the church by Malcolm, Earl of Fife, in the twelfth century, and a group of Cistercian monks from Kinross settled there at the beginning of the thirteenth century. The remains of the Abbey's central tower and vaulted choir have been preserved in the Abbey church which was restored in 1633.

An important and prominent citizen of Culross was George Bruce, who was granted the right to mine coal on the Abbey land in a charter of 1575. He developed new seams, some far out beneath the Forth, and devised new machinery for draining the mines.

Culross Palace was built by George Bruce at the end of the sixteenth century. It is a fine example of a merchant's house in the traditional Scottish style, with crowstepped gables and random rubble walls, whilst inside there are fine painted ceilings. In 1611 the mine was visited by James VI, at which time he knighted Bruce and stayed at the Palace. Bruce was also responsible for establishing a flourishing trade in coal and salt from Culross to the Netherlands. Shortly before Bruce died in 1642 the coal mine was flooded during a terrible

Culross Palace.

storm. The Town House was built in 1626 and the clock tower was added in 1783. Today this is the local centre of the National Trust for Scotland which has been instrumental in restoring this unique and remarkable seventeenth-century mercantile and mining community. Within this centre the NTS has a continuous film show together with many fine books and publications about the town.

Now carry on along the B9037 in an easterly direction towards the two Valleyfield villages.

High and Low Valleyfield were two communities that sprang up at the end of the nineteenth century to house the miners who worked at the Valleyfield Colliery on the foreshore of the River Forth. On 28 October 1939 at 3.45 a.m., a terrible disaster happened at this colliery, when an explosion occurred deep underground. It was thought to have been caused initially by explosives used in shot-firing, but the fire spread rapidly due to a build-up of fire-damp, engulfing the Diamond section of the pit deep under the Forth and destroying it completely. All 35 men working there at the time were killed. Most were burned to death, but a few were killed by the concussive effect of the terrible blast. Thirty of the men, mostly young, were married, some with large families. Even today the local people still remember this terrible disaster.

After passing Low and High Valleyfield the route continues along the B9037 past the small villages of Newmills and Torryburn and on to the roundabout at the junction with the busy A985 trunk road. Taking extreme care, exit by the second road, which is the minor road signposted to Oakley.

Cycle along this road for 3 km to its end at a T-junction. Here turn right and within a few metres go under a railway bridge. On the other side of this bridge turn right and rejoin the cycle route. Retrace this route back to Dunfermline.

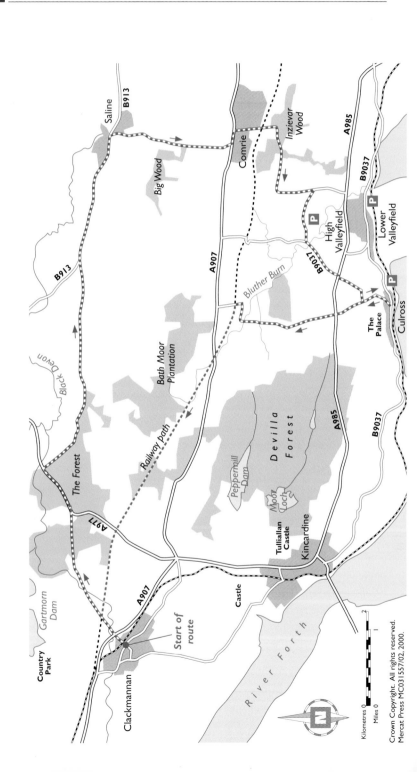

# CLACKMANNAN TO CULROSS

Clackmannan was made a Royal Burgh by King William the Lion. The area was in the hands of the Earls of Annandale, who were part of the Bruce family, and it is believed that King David II, the son of King Robert I (Robert the Bruce), lived in the castle at Clackmannan for a time. It is not known what happened to this castle but it was probably replaced by the present tower in the fourteenth century, for around it there are signs of earlier buildings.

The Clack Mannan (stone of Mannan) can be seen seated on a high plinth at the Town Cross next to the Tolbooth and the Mercat Cross. Mannan was the name of the Celtic sea god and is also the basis of the names of Slamannan, Dalmeny and the Isle of Man. According to legend the stone originally lay at the edge of a loch in an area to the south of the village known as Lookaboutye, and was moved into the village itself by Robert the Bruce.

The route begins outside the Tolbooth in Main Street. Start off along this road in an easterly direction, past the Library gifted by Andrew Carnegie, to the junction with Alloa Road and carry straight on over this junction to the B910 signposted for Kinross. Carry on under the A907, after which the road begins to climb, slowly at first and then becoming steeper, for 3 km to the junction with the A977 and turn left.

Take care on the kilometre of the route that uses this busy road as it continues uphill into Forest Mill. At Forest Mill there is a pottery and coffee shop which is worth a visit, particularly after the exertion of the previous 3 km. Outside the pottery there is a minor road signposted to

## INFORMATION

**Distance:** 37 km (22 miles) circular route.

**Map:** OS Landranger, sheets 58 and 65; Kingdom of Fife Cycle Ways West Fife map.

**Start and finish:** There are no public car parks in Clackmannan, so the route begins outside the Town Hall in Main Street.

**Terrain:** Very hilly in places, with prolonged uphill stretches between Clackmannan and Forest Mill.

**Refreshments:** Available from places in Clackmannan, Culross and the Pottery at Forest Mill.

Clackmannan Tolbooth and Merkat Cross.

Clackmannan Castle.

Saline. Carry on along this road into Fife for 5 km, until you reach the junction of the B913. Here turn right and take this road the remaining 3 km into Saline.

Saline is a former weaving village with many interesting eighteenth-century cottages which have survived despite the extensive development of mining in the neighbourhood during the nineteenth and twentieth centuries. It was often visited by Sir Walter Scott who stayed at nearby North Kinneddar, the home of his friend William Erskine, Lord Kinneddar, to whom he dedicated the Third Canto of his poem *Marmion*.

On entering Saline the junction of West and North Road is soon reached. Turn right into the North Road and then almost immediately turn right again into Oakley Road, heading south under the cycleway and out of the village. After a little under a kilometre turn right and take the minor road which joins the B9037. Once this has been reached, turn left and head for Culross. At the junction with the very busy A985 turn right and then immediately left on to the minor road signposted for Culross. Within 1 km this beautiful and historic village is reached. Take time to look around before commencing the return journey. (A description of Culross is given in Route 1.)

For the return journey retrace the route out of Culross, past the Abbey and along Gallows Loan out of the village. After about 200 m there is a junction. Carry straight on along this minor road which climbs to the junction with the A985. Cross this and continue for 2 km to West Grange, looking out for the point where the road you are on passes over a bridge, below which the cycle track runs along the track bed of the former railway. Next to the far-right edge of the bridge, as you are facing it, is a rough, unmade and steep path down to the Clackmannan to Dunfermline cycleway. Take the cycleway in a westerly direction for the remaining 8 km to its end at the B910. Turn left on to this road and within about 200 m the junction with Alloa Road is reached. Carry on straight ahead into Cattle Market and then on into the High Street and the end of the route.

Town House, Culross.

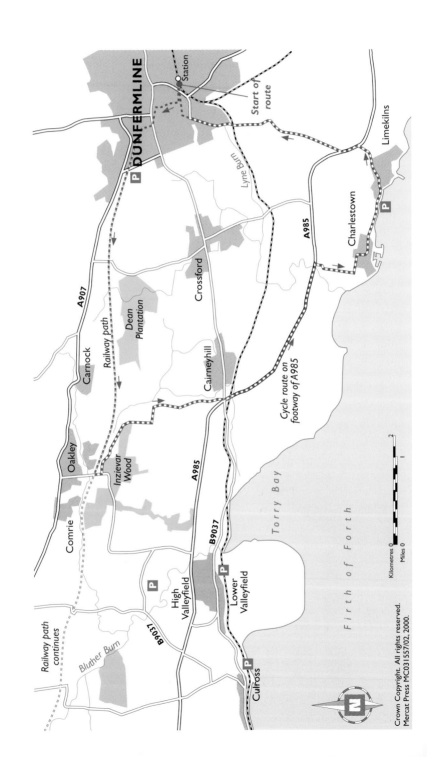

# DUNFERMLINE TO CHARLESTOWN

Leave the station area and carry on through an underpass which links the station with Comely Park. Travel in a westerly direction to the junction with New Road and carry straight on into Priory Lane. After 200 m or so the road sweeps round to the left. Here carry straight on in a westerly direction, into a narrower street which is still Priory Lane. Turn right at the T-junction, where Andrew Carnegie's birthplace is situated, into St Margaret Street. Turn first left into Monastery Street which becomes St Catherine's Wynd. Turn left into Bridge Street and carry straight on over the four-way junction into Chalmers Street. At the end of this street turn left into Golfdrum Street which ends at William Street. Here turn right and carry on for 200 m to where the access to the cycleway is reached. Turn left into an area laid out as a car park, at the end of which the cycleway begins in a westerly direction.

**INFORMATION**

**Distance:** 22 km (13.7 miles) circular route.

**Map:** OS Landranger, sheet 59; Kingdom of Fife Cycle Ways West Fife map.

**Start and finish:** Dunfermline Railway Station.

**Terrain:** Fairly flat and easy.

**Refreshments:** Available from many places in Dunfermline and also in Oakley, Charlestown and Limekilns.

Carry on along this clearly defined cycle path for 6 km to Oakley. At Oakley leave the cycle path and carry on down to Station Road and turn left. Within a few metres go under a railway bridge and then carry on for another few metres to the first junction on the left and turn on to this road. Carry on for 3 km to its end at the roundabout at the junction of the A985 and A994. Taking extreme care, exit the roundabout by the second road, the A985, and proceed along the southern footway, which has been constructed for cyclists and pedestrians. Carry on along this footway for 3 km to the junction which is signposted for Charlestown. Turn right here and head down West Road into Charlestown.

St Catherine's Wynd, Dunfermline.

Charlestown is a planned village founded in 1770 by Charles, 5th Earl of Elgin (1732–1771). It was built as an industrial village to house the families of the coal miners and limestone quarriers who were brought in from other areas to carry out this work. The village became a Conservation Area in 1974.

Charlestown Harbour.

Between Charlestown and Limekilns, set out on lands once owned by the monastery at Dunfermline, lies Broomhall House, the seat of the Earls of Elgin and Kincardine. This estate was once owned by Robert Richardson, Treasurer to Mary, Queen of Scots. It was purchased in 1600 by Sir George Bruce, who changed the name to Broomhall. This illustrious family are the closest living descendants of Robert the Bruce.

There are two other members of this family who deserve a mention. The first is Thomas, 7th Earl of Elgin, who at the beginning of the nineteenth century, whilst Greece was under Turkish Rule, shortly before the War of Independence, held the post of British Ambassador to Turkey. He sent a team to Athens to draw its monuments and make casts for the decoration of Broomhall House. The international political situation of the time allowed the Earl later to remove many statues and friezes from the Parthenon and other sites around central Greece, the Aegean Islands and Asia Minor, where Greek civilisation had once flourished. These were all eventually sent back to Britain where they still remain to this day. Known as the Elgin Marbles, they form one of the British Museum's most important collections. A discussion of the ethics of the Earl's actions is firmly beyond the scope of this book.

The second notable member of the family was James Bruce, 8th Earl of Elgin, who was the Governor-General of Canada between 1847 and 1854. He then went on to become the Viceroy of India in 1861.

At Broomhall there are relics of Robert the Bruce. A large two-handed sword and a helmet are displayed, both said to have been borne by Bruce at the Battle of Bannockburn in 1314. Broomhall is not open to the public.

View over Charlestown.

At the end of West Road turn right into Rocks Road and follow this around at right angles to join Main Street which soon becomes Promenade. Carry on along Promenade to Church Street, where the village of Limekilns starts.

Once press-gangs would have roamed the streets of this ancient seaport on the lookout for unlucky men to serve on the ships of the local fleet. The harbour was developed as a port by the medieval merchants of Dunfermline who exported lime, salt and coal, and imported wood, wine and glassware. Limekilns also had a soap and rope works, saltpans and a brewery. Limekilns' oldest building is the sixteenth-century King's Cellar in Academy Square. Part of this building was originally built by the monks of Dunfermline in the fourteenth century for storing wine and other imported goods. The village was created a Conservation Area in 1984.

Continue along Church Street, which becomes Dunfermline Road, and after 300 m the junction with the A985 is reached. Turn left on to this busy road and cycle along it for about 400 m, taking extreme care, to the junction with the B9156 signposted for Dunfermline. Take this road for 3 km all the way into Dunfermline, entering the town at Limekilns Road, which goes on to become Forth Street. At the end of this street turn right into Nethertown Road and at the traffic-signalled, four-way junction turn left into Moodie Street and then turn right into Priory Lane. Carry straight on into Comely Park, at the end of which is the underpass back into the Station Forecourt and the end of the route.

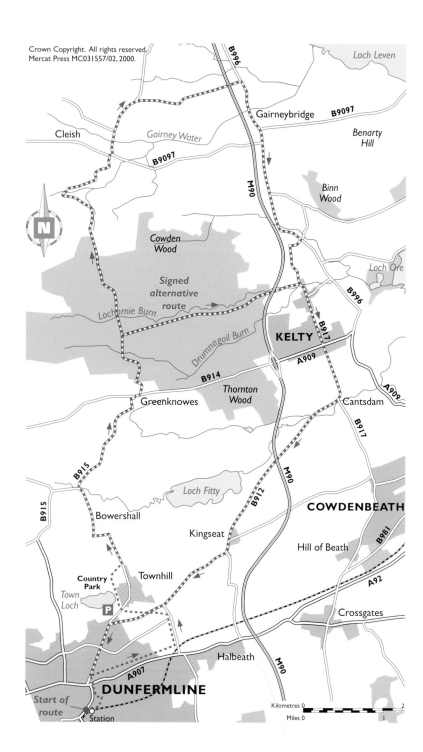

# DUNFERMLINE TO KELTY

L eave Dunfermline Railway Station from platform two and enter the small car park. At the east end of it there is a Kingdom of Fife cycle sign. Follow this into St Margaret's Park. This Park takes its name from St Margaret, the wife of King Malcolm III (Malcolm Canmore), whose reformation of the Scottish church is described in Route 1. Malcolm and Margaret lived out most of their lives in Dunfermline and both are buried in the Abbey.

Set off along the path to the right and follow the cycle signs, first of all the one to the Forth Road Bridge. After about 100 m there is a junction: here follow the signs for Kinross to the left.

The path then starts to ascend in a northerly direction towards a shelter and a fountain at the top of the hill diagonally across the park. At this point stop and look back, for there is a panoramic view over the River Forth, with the Naval Dockyard at Rosyth, the Forth Bridges, Bo'ness and the Bathgate Hills all clearly visible. Continue downhill on this path to Appin Crescent, where a Toucan Crossing is located, and cross to the other side of the road. From here take the cycle path which carries on in a northerly direction for a short distance before turning east to where it connects with a small car park. Here turn right and continue to follow the cycle signs to Kinross along Leys Park Road. Soon another cycle path is reached which passes close to East End Park, the home of Dunfermline Academicals Football Club. After passing through a gate, this well-constructed and well-lit cycle path continues for a kilometre to Whitefield Road and Dunfermline Queen Margaret Station, which was opened in January 2000. From here the route continues north along the west footway of this road, still following the cycle signs for Kinross. The route carries on along

### INFORMATION

**Distance:** 35 km (21.8 miles) circular route.

**Map:** OS Landranger, sheet 59; Kingdom of Fife Cycle Ways West Fife map.

**Start and finish:** Dunfermline Railway Station.

**Terrain:** Flat at the beginning followed by undulating sections and some prolonged climbs.

**Refreshments:** Available from places in Dunfermline and Kelty.

Modern cycling technology—a Toucan crossing in Dunfermline.

this footway, which has now been designated a cycling and pedestrian footway, for almost a kilometre, past the West Fife General Hospital, to where another cycle path begins, heading in a westerly direction. This cycle path, like the previous one, follows the line of a dismantled railway for 2 km, skirting Townhill Country Park which has Town Loch as its main feature, and emerges on to the minor road at the north end of Townhill.

Cleish Hill.

Turn left on to this road and carry on uphill, taking care at the two 90-degree bends on this stretch of road. The road passes through the small village of Bowershall before joining with the B915. At this junction turn right and carry on through the Valley of Balmule where there is an interesting woodlands initiative being carried out. Carry on along the B915 for 2 km to the junction with the B914 and turn right. Within 100 m turn left on to a minor road following the signs for Cleish. Once on this road the route winds uphill through woodland for about 1½ km to where there is a green cycle sign to Blairadam Forest and Kelty. This forest track is a considerable short cut, for the route described here is 10 km to Kelty. So choose for yourself.

Following the cycle signs to Kinross and Strathmiglo, carry on up the steep hill for 2 km to the top. Here you will be glad you made the effort to climb this high because the view over Loch Leven to the edge of the Lomond Hills is breathtaking. The winding road then begins to descend very steeply, so take care. As the road drops past the Nivingston Craigs with its rocky outcropped face, a burn cascades gurgling and tumbling down the hillside, gathering momentum on its way to join the Gairney Water before it gushes into Loch Leven. After passing Nivingston Country House and Restaurant you will reach a road junction. With the hills now left behind, turn right here and within a few metres Cleich Mill and the junction with the B9097 is reached. Turn left and follow the cycle sign for Crook of Devon, and, after 700 m, as the main road turns left, carry straight on to a minor road, once again following the cycle route to Kinross. After 800 m take the right fork on to an even more minor road. Now, leaving the cycle route behind, follow this road to the T-junction with the B996 and turn right, following the signs for Cowdenbeath. After a short distance a noble column is reached. This was erected to commemorate the formation of the first presbytery of the first Secession of clergy from the Church of Scotland in 1733.

Snowdrops by the wayside.

Continue along the B996 for 3½ km to a junction with a minor road, which is signposted on the right to Keltybridge. Turn on to it. Carry on through the picturesque little village of Keltybridge and on to the junction with Main Street (B917) at the edge of Kelty. Turn right and follow this road all the way through this former mining town. Cycle across Station Road (A909), on to Oakfield Street and continue out of town. After just over a kilometre, turn right on to the B912 for Dunfermline. Follow this road uphill for a short distance and then carry on over the motorway and past Loch Fitty with its Trout Farm on the right. Go on through the village of Kingseat. At the junction where the B912 turns to the left, following the road to the General Hospital, carry straight on down Kingseat Road to the junction of Townhill Road. Then turn right into Townhill Road and follow it all the way to its end. Turn left at the traffic lights into Leys Park Road, join the cycle route and retrace this route back through St Margaret's Park to the station.

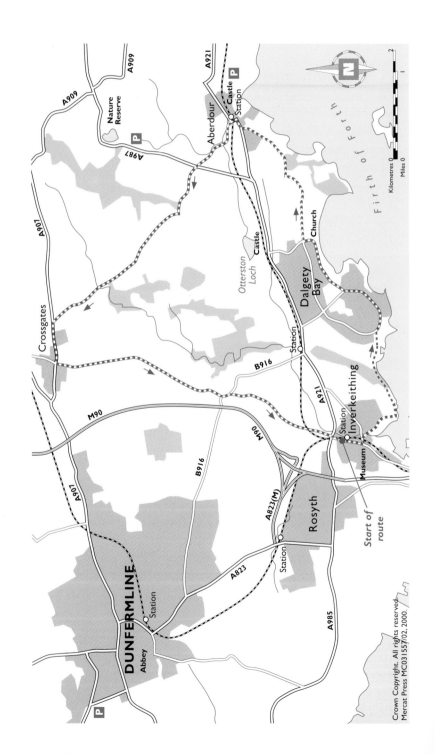

# INVERKEITHING TO CROSSGATES VIA ABERDOUR

I nverkeithing is an ancient Royal Burgh, in fact it is one of the oldest in Scotland, with char- ters granted by William the Lion and Robert III in 1139 and 1399.

The town contains a host of ancient buildings, in- cluding St Peter's Parish Church in Church Street, the tower of which dates back to the fourteenth century. Possibly dating from the same period is the Franciscan Friary in Queen Street, the *hospitium* (guest house) of which now houses the town's museum. The garden at the rear has a beauti- ful view over the old harbour, which was developed in the early part of the seventeenth century as a port for the transportation of coal and salt to the Netherlands. The oldest dwelling-house in the town is Rosebery House in King Street, which dates from the first quarter of the sixteenth century.

The Tolbooth in Town Hall Street, formerly Tolbooth Street, is the second building of that ilk to occupy this site. Its inscribed bell is from the first building. The present Tolbooth dates from 1754 and was designed to house a debtors' prison in the top floor, the courtroom in the middle floor and the 'black hole' or prison in the ground floor. Later, as the street name now suggests, it was used as the Town Hall. Outside stood the sixteenth-century Mercat Cross, which, alas, has now been moved to a totally unsuitable location at the end of Bank Street. I surmise this was done to suit the needs of the motor vehicle.

In 1651, at the battle of Inverkeithing, about a mile to the north of the town, Oliver

## INFORMATION

**Distance:** 20 km (12.5 miles) circular route.

**Map:** OS Landranger, sheet 65; Kingdom of Fife Cycle Ways Kingdom Route map.

**Start and finish:** Inverkeithing Railway Station.

**Terrain:** From Inverkeithing to Aberdour along the Fife Coastal Path is fairly flat. The remainder is undulat- ing with some short stretches of steeper gradients.

**Refreshments:** Available from many places in Inverkeithing and Aberdour.

Rosebery House, Inverkeithing.

Cromwell's troops defeated a mixed force of Royalist Highlanders and pressed townspeople. The latter had no stomach for a fight and quickly fled back to the town: as a reprisal, after the battle was over, Cromwell's troops returned to the town, sacking and burning it.

Leave Inverkeithing Railway Station, proceed to Chapel Place and turn left. Follow this road as it becomes High Street, then turn left into Heriot Street and left again into King Street. Turn right and follow the Kingdom of Fife Cycle Route signs, first into Commercial Road and then left into Preston Crescent, at the end of which the cycle route shares its route with the Fife Coastal Path.

A typical signpost in Inverkeithing for the Kingdom of Fife Cycle Route.

The route continues past the vast Prestonhill Quarry which is no longer in use. It then assumes a more rural setting until it reaches St David's Bay where the housing estates of Dalgety Bay begin. Dalgety Bay, now a town in its own right, was created in 1965 and has grown constantly ever since. Still following the Kingdom of Fife Cycle Route signs for Inverkeithing, at this point it is necessary to leave the path and join the adjacent roads for a few hundred metres of the route. Once back on the Coastal Path the route passes Donibristle House. This house, built in the seventeenth century, was the home of the 5th and 6th Earls of Moray and was partially burned down in the mid-nineteenth century. It occupies the site of a previous castle which also belonged to the Earls of Moray. It was at the earlier castle, in 1592, that James Stewart, the Bonnie Earl of Moray, was murdered for his ultra-Protestant views by the Earl of Huntly.

Carry on for some distance to the ruins of St Bridget's Kirk, the main structure of which dates from 1244. After the Reformation flanking aisles were added by a number of families, with sitting areas above the burial vaults; the grandest of these was built by the Seton family at the west end in

1610. It has a small drawing-room off the loft, which is reached by a small, semi-octagonal stairway.

The route continues past Braefoot Bay, a deep-water tanker terminal which handles Ethylene piped down from Mossmoran Natural Gas Liquefication Plant, 6 km to the north.

Along this stretch of the route a good view can be had over the Firth of Forth to Inchcolm Island, with its Augustinian abbey founded by Alexander I in about 1223. Most of the abbey buildings date from the thirteenth to the fifteenth centuries. In the fourteenth century Walter Bower, abbot at Incholm, wrote the *Scotichronicon*, an epic history of the Scottish people from earliest times. This circulated in manuscript form for centuries, but a modern edition in nine volumes has recently been published. The monastery was abandoned at the Reformation, but the buildings are still remarkably intact. The island is accessible by boat from Hawes Pier, South Queensferry, and the round trip takes about two and a half hours.

The route now skirts Aberdour Golf Course, through Dovecot Park. At the end of the Park turn right into the High Street and then left into Station Road.

Aberdour consists of Easter Aberdour and Wester Aberdour, the two being separated by the Dour Burn. Right in the

Inchcolm Island in the Forth, with St Colm's Abbey.

middle between the eastern and western parts stands Aberdour Castle, which was built by the mighty Douglas family in 1342. The castle remained in their possession until it was accidentally set on fire and then abandoned in the eighteenth century. Within the Castle grounds is the much older parish church of St Fillans, which dates from the twelfth century. This church was abandoned about 200 years ago, but restored in 1926. Today Aberdour is a very popular holiday resort. Its harbour, once used extensively by local fishing boats, now provides a sheltered anchorage for yachts of all shapes and sizes. As its name suggests, Silversands Bay has a beautiful beach which offers the safest swimming along the Fife coast.

At this point the reader has two choices. The first, which is described next, is to continue on inland on the hilly road to Crossgates, from where you can return to Inverkeithing. The second is simply to retrace the route you have taken along the Fife Coastal Path, with a second chance to see the many interesting places that this route offers.

Once in Station Place, within a few metres a junction is reached. Here the cycle signs point right, towards the Fife coastal towns. However, our route is straight on, taking the minor road to Crossgates. This road soon begins to climb, and after a kilometre or so reaches the junction with the B9157. Here, carry straight on across the junction, keeping to the minor road to Crossgates. This road continues to forge its way uphill, gradually for the most part, but within the section are a couple of fairly short but very steep stretches. If that wasn't enough to contend with, there are also a couple of hairpin bends to be negotiated. This road only lasts for 5 km, and when the junction with the A907 at Fordell is reached, the uphill stretch is over.

Turn left on to this road for 500 m and proceed into Crossgates. Here turn left on to the B981 and, remembering the old adage 'what goes up must come down', follow this road as it descends for some 6 km back down to Inverkeithing. On this stretch of road there are good views over the River Forth and its road and rail bridges. The latter part of this road has a cycle lane on both sides of it. So simply keep to this lane and follow the cycle signs for Aberdour into Inverkeithing. At the double roundabout at the junction with the A921 the

An unusual view of the Forth Rail Bridge.

route reverts to the footway. Follow this route into Chapel Place and thus back to Inverkeithing Station.

As an alternative to the starting and finishing point of this route, by following the clearly defined Kingdom of Fife Cycle Route signs along the B981, one could start and finish at North Queensferry or even cross the Forth Road Bridge into West Lothian—or, as another choice, go on into the centre of Edinburgh using a part of the North Sea Cycle Route.

Looking across Braefoot Bay to the two Forth Bridges.

The cycle route across the Forth Road Bridge is something to wonder at. Pause opposite one of the two main towers of the bridge, which are 156 m high, to marvel at the engineering of this magnificent structure and imagine what it would have been like to be a steel erector working precariously so high above the mighty river. Or pause at the centre of the bridge, 50 m above the river, and take in the splendid views over Fife and the Lothians.

North Queensferry, which is much smaller than its counterpart on the other side of the Firth of Forth, was until the opening of the Forth Road Bridge the northern landing stage of the ferry from South Queensferry, a ferry which had been in existence, in various forms, for almost 900 years.

The town reflects its ancient past, with many of its buildings dating back hundreds of years. A full account of these can be found in a leaflet published by North Queensferry Heritage Trust. In the nineteenth century this town enjoyed popularity as a tourist resort, as it provided a safe bay to swim in. Recently, thanks in part to the opening of the aquarium 'Deep Sea World', with its wonderful transparent viewing tunnel on the seabed, the town has become very popular once more.

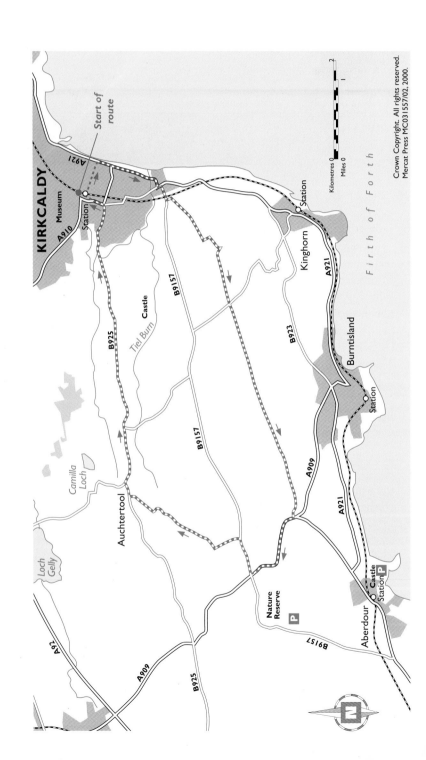

KIRKCALDY

Start of route

A921

Museum

A910

Station

B925

Tiel Burn

Castle

B9157

B9157

Camilla Loch

Loch Gelly

Auchtertool

A92

A909

B925

Nature Reserve

B9157

Aberdour

Castle
Station

A921

A909

A921

B923

Burntisland

Station

Kinghorn

Station

Firth of Forth

Kilometres 0        1        2
Miles 0

# KIRKCALDY TO AUCHTERTOOL

Kirkcaldy is the largest town in Fife, with a population of 47,930. It is known as the 'Lang Toun', for it stretches out in a wide arc along the coast of the Firth of Forth from Linktown to Dysart. Kirkcaldy became a burgh under the administration of Dunfermline Abbey in 1304, and was given a royal charter by Charles II in 1664. The town then became a centre for trade because of its deep harbour. However, Kirkcaldy's growth was hastened by the advent of the Industrial Revolution, and it expanded rapidly in the nineteenth century with the development of its linoleum, textile and coal industries. The linoleum industry continued well into the twentieth century and at its height was notorious for a lingering aroma which pervaded the town.

The most famous of all political economists, Adam Smith (1723–90), was born in Kirkcaldy. He became the Professor of Logic at the University of Glasgow, and went on to write *The Wealth of Nations* which is, to this day, considered one of the greatest works of political economy.

The famous eighteenth-century architect Robert Adam, with his brothers James and John, were all born in the town. Robert created a style based on classical architecture and was architect to King George III. He designed many of the buildings of the New Town in Edinburgh.

Ravenscraig Castle is situated at the southern end of Ravenscraig Park off the Dysart Road. Begun by King James II in 1460, this was the first castle in Scotland to have been built with artillery defences, all of which face landward. This castle is worth taking time to visit.

On leaving the railway station, turn left on to Whytemelville Road and head south to the bottom of the hill using the cycle lanes. At the traffic signals

Dovecot at Ravenscraig Castle.

turn left, using the advanced stop lines for cyclists, and then turn immediately right into West Fergus Place. Still using the cycle lanes, carry on down past the junction of High Street into Charlotte Street. Take the cycle access, which is straight ahead of you as you reach the bottom of Charlotte Street, into Cowan Street which leads to Esplanade. Cross this at the pedestrian crossing and then turn right and head up a ramp on to a raised area. After crossing this diagonally to the other side, proceed down the ramp on to the promenade and head south.

Almost at the end of the promenade there is a car park. Here, following the cycle signs, cycle on to the east footway of Esplanade, cross this road using the centre island and carry on into Heggies Wynd. Turn left into Link Street and follow the cycle lanes to the junction at Bridge Street. Here turn left and then first right into Invertiel Terrace. Go uphill into this small housing estate and carry on to the end of the road. Here follow the cycle signs left on to the cyclepath and continue for about 100 m to the footway of Invertiel Road. The stadium that can be seen on the right of the cyclepath belongs to Raith Rovers, Kirkcaldy's own football team. Here turn left under the railway bridge and cross this road into Tyrie Road. Once on this minor road proceed uphill and into open country.

View of Kirkcaldy.

This road ascends gradually for a kilometre into the countryside with a combination of farm and seascape. Pass the ancient ruined tower a kilometre to the right, known as Pitteadie Castle. As you head along this stretch of road, stop and take in the fine view across the Forth Estuary.

After about 9 km head straight across a four-way junction and thereafter look out for the ancient standing stones in a field on the right. One can only imagine what rituals were performed here by the ancient folk who erected these monoliths.

After 12 km the highest point of this road is reached and there are more splendid views over West Fife and the River Forth, including its two beautiful bridges and the clutch of small islands including Inchcolm and Inchmickery.

At the T-junction with the A909 turn right and follow this main road for about a kilometre to the junction. (Although this is an 'A' road it is seldom very busy. However, keep a careful eye out for fast-moving vehicles and do take care.) On the right of this road is Dunearn Country Woodland and the Stenhouse Reservoir.

Turn right at the junction with the B9157 signposted for Kirkcaldy. Go along this road for a little less than a kilometre and turn left on to the minor road signposted for Auchtertool. This very pleasant but narrow minor road has some rather acute turns, so take care. Turn right at the T-junction on to the B925, and after 200 m the village of Auchtertool is reached.

Auchtertool once stood at the junction of the roads linking Dunfermline to Kirkcaldy and the Kinghorn ferry to Perth. These roads are, to a great extent, still in existence today, but are now minor roads and used by the cycle routes. Auchtertool once had a thriving distillery, but today the village is mainly agricultural.

Proceed through the village and then start to climb, sometimes quite steeply, for a kilometre. After another 3 km the outskirts of Kirkcaldy are reached and the town entered at Boglily Road. Once at the end of this road turn left at the roundabout, following signs for the station. Go along Abbotshall Road, then take the right fork, still keeping on this road, and turn left into Whytemelville Road. At the top of this the station entrance marks the end of the route.

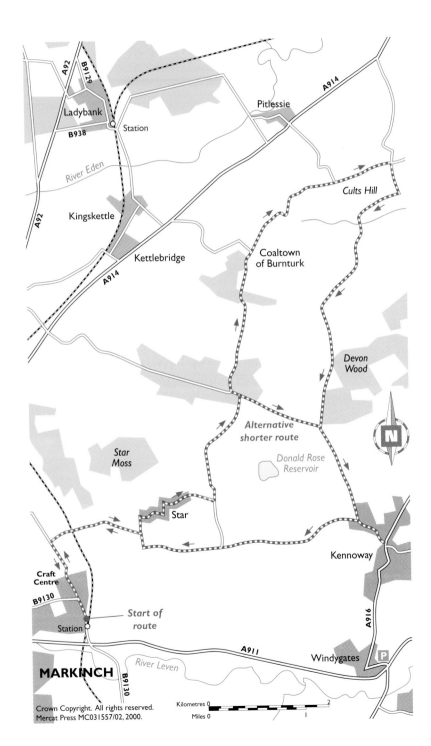

# MARKINCH TO KENNOWAY

The name Markinch is Celtic in origin and means an island in the middle of a bog. This Celtic connection certainly would lend support to the assertion that it was the largest settlement of one of the provinces of Pictland. There are terraces on Markinch Hill which are thought by some to be Roman in origin. However, this is highly unlikely, as the local indigenous population at the time was Pictish, and although many tribes thoughout southern Scotland lived together in peace with the Romans, this was not the case with the Picts. Indeed, there was constant aggravation between them. This fact alone makes it much more likely that these terraces are medieval. At the northern end of the town on Hill Terrace stands the ancient Celtic Stob Cross which may have marked the limits of sanctuary of Markinch Church.

This parish church stands on the site of a preaching centre said to have been established towards the end of the sixth century by St Drostan, a nephew of St Columba, and overlooks the centre of Markinch.

## INFORMATION

**Distance:** 16 km (10 miles) circular route (with a further 10 km if continuing to Cults Mill).

**Map:** OS Landranger, sheet 59; Kingdom of Fife Cycle Ways Kingdom Route and Glenrothes maps.

**Start and finish:** Markinch Railway Station.

**Terrain:** The shorter route is almost flat, the longer route being undulating. Neither is difficult.

**Refreshments:** Available in Markinch and Kennoway.

Markinch Parish Church.

Markinch Railway Station.

Leave the station, which is a Tudor Italianate build-ing dating from the opening of the first railway through Fife in 1847, and head north into High Street. Carry straight on into Glass Street and then go round St Drostan's Parish Church, on the one-way-street system, along Kirk Street and into Stobcross Road. Open country is soon reached. Within a kilometre there is T-junction: turn right here and follow the Kingdom of Fife Cycle Route signs for Star. This road then begins to climb gradu-ally for a short time. At the next junction keep following the Cycle Route signs to the left, for Star and Ceres, and carry on into the small village of Star.

After leaving this small village turn left at the next junction, still following the cycle signs. At the next-again junction a decision has to be made as to what length and type of cycle run you wish to take. If you want a longer and more hilly run, then con-tinue to follow the cycle signs through Coaltown of Burnturk and around Cults Hill. Carry on along the signed Cycle Route for 5 km to the four-way junction, and follow the signs for Kennoway, which is a further 6 km further on. On the other hand, if you want a much shorter run then turn right, leaving the signed Cycle Route, and complete the 3 km into Kennoway.

The small town of Kennoway, like Markinch, also has an ancient past, for it, too, was a Pictish settlement. To the south of the present town is the Pictish motte known as Maiden Castle, which would have given protection to the inhabitants of the surrounding area. Later this area be-

Rural view along the route.

longed to the Priory of St Andrews, and a church was built here by the monks and dedicated to St Kenneth. This is the likely origin of the town's name. In the present parish church, built in 1851, is the oldest surviving Communion Cup in Scotland, dating from 1671. The town prospered throughout the Middle Ages due to its location on the main road between the ferries of the Firth of Forth and Firth of Tay. This prosperity was continued by the development of the weaving industry. Today the town is mainly a residential area for people who work in the commercial and industrial centres close by.

Once in Kennoway turn right at the T-junction where it is signposted for Star and Markinch. Follow this pleasant road for 4 km until it reaches the junction with the road to Star, turn left and retrace the route back into Markinch.

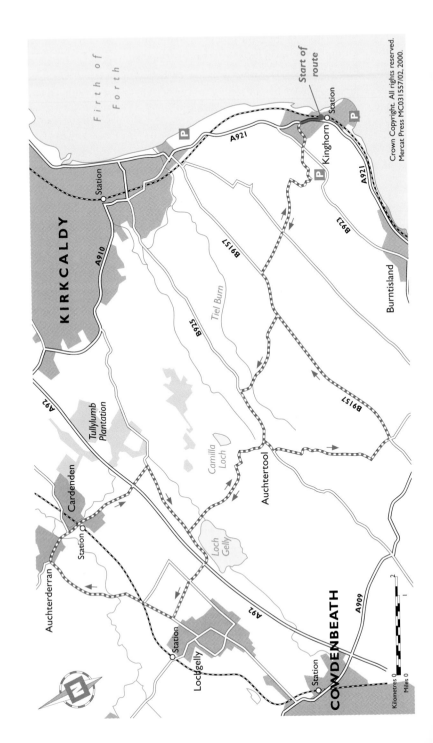

# KINGHORN TO LOCHGELLY

**K**inghorn, as its name might suggest, has a great and royal past. Its first association with royalty was when Macbeth repelled the Vikings at the battle of Kinghorn in 1040. On his succession to the throne of Scotland in 1165, King William I ('the Lion') declared Kinghorn a Royal Burgh and built a castle here. Two centuries later the castle was gifted by Robert II to his son-in-law Sir John Lyon, whose descendent was created Earl of Kinghorn and later Strathmore in 1606. However, today no trace of this castle exists. To the west of Kinghorn a roadside cross erected in 1886 commemorates Alexander III, who fell to his death from the cliff-top here in March 1286. It was Alexander who once again repelled the Vikings, this time at the Battle of Largs in 1263.

In the Middle Ages Kinghorn became a busy and thriving place, thanks to the introduction of a ferry link with the Lothians. It later went on to become a centre of spinning and shipbuilding.

Leave the station and turn left uphill on Station Brae. Turn left again into Rossland Road, which

## INFORMATION

**Distance:** 30 km (18.7 miles) circular route.

**Map:** OS Landranger, sheets 58, 59 and 66; Kingdom of Fife Cycle Ways Kingdom Route map.

**Start and finish:** Kinghorn Railway Station.

**Terrain:** After the first 3 km where the steeper hills are encountered, the rest of the route is generally undulating.

**Refreshments:** Available in Kinghorn, Lochgelly and Cardenden.

Looking over Kinghorn Bay.

is a one-way street, and immediately turn right around the island and then turn right into High Street. Proceed through the centre of town noticing that the name of the street changes to St Leonard's Place. Turn left into North Overgate and head uphill. At the end of this street continue left into Townhead, which in turn becomes Kilcruik Road. At the junction with the B923 carry on straight over into the minor road signposted for Auchtertool. After a short distance the road starts to climb through Red Path Brae. Take care as there are two acute bends to negotiate on this steep stretch of road. After you have cycled on this minor road for about 500 m the elevation has gone from almost sea level to 103 m, so take a break and look at the fine view over the Firth of Forth.

Autumn colours in Fife.

Go on now another kilometre to a four-way junction and carry straight on. After a short incline the road levels out somewhat. Continue for a kilometre to the junction of the B9157 and turn left. Carry on along this road for 500 m and then turn right, once again on to a minor road signposted for Auchtertool. Cycle along this undulating road for 1½ km to the junction with the B925, turn left and soon the village of Auchtertool is reached. Continue till you come to a crossroads and take the right fork on to the minor road signposted for Lochgelly.

On this pleasant stretch of rural road it is hard to imagine how close one is to the industrial heartland of Fife, until, that is, one turns a particular corner. Here is a view to the valley below where the vast chemical works close to the town of Cowdenbeath is situated. However, even at this point, history is never far away, for in the field close to the road are the ruins of Hallyards Castle or Mansion, which was built by King James V's Lord High Treasurer, Sir James Kirkcaldy of Grange.

Carry further on along this road and Loch Gelly is soon located. This is where Fife Water-ski Club have their base and there is always plenty of activity on the loch, particularly at weekends.

At the T-junction turn left and carry on to a roundabout and take the B9149 past another roundabout and on to a third: if you turn left here the small town of Lochgelly is reached.

The name Lochgelly perhaps has the effect of producing an ice-cold feeling of terror in the hearts of the over-35-year-olds reading this. For Lochgelly was the place where the infamous leather belt or tawse was manufactured. This instrument of torture was used to great effect by many school teachers on wayward pupils, and the author remembers well, on many occasions, the pain of the maximum punishment, which was 'six of the best'.

Lochgelly was once a small agricultural market centre. It prospered as a mining town during the

I'm making haste to leave Lochgelly behind!

period between the granting of mineral rights to the Lochgelly Iron and Coal Company in the 1830s and the closure of local pits in the 1960s. Lochgelly is the highest town in Fife and was designated a burgh in 1876.

From this third roundabout the route continues on to the B981 in the direction of Auchterderran and Cardenden 3 km to the east. After passing Lochgelly cemetery, where perhaps the man who invented the torture-instrument of Scottish school children is buried, enter Auchterderran on Jamphlars Road.

A fine day for cycling.

Cardenden is a former mining town on the Garden Burn. It is made up of the small communities of Auchterderran, Bowhill and Dundonald, and was the home of the dramatist Joe Corrie (1894–1968) who gives his name to the Corrie Centre. Cardenden was also the birthplace, in 1960, of award-winning crime writer Ian Rankin. So watch out for Inspector Rebus.

Sport, too, has figured largely in Cardenden's history, with the Old Firm, Celtic and Rangers, to the forefront. The celebrated John Thomson, born in Kirkcaldy in 1909, lived at Bowhill, Cardenden. He became goalkeeper for Glasgow Celtic Football Club and also had a distinguished international career. He died at the tender age of 22 as a result of injuries accidentally received during a game against his team's great rivals, Rangers, at Ibrox Park in Glasgow. The player who so tragically killed him in what was an unfortunate accident never again kicked a ball. Such was Thomson's fame that tens of thousands of people attended his funeral at Bowhill, where he is buried. Although this accident happened almost three-quarters of a century ago, to this day there are still many tributes left at his memorial in Cardenden.

At the junction with Main Street turn right, follow this road into Station Road and continue along to where this main road turns left into Cardenden Road. Here carry straight on ahead, staying on Station Road, proceed under the railway bridge into Main

The Thomson Memorial, Cardenden.

Road and continue uphill and out of town. Soon the flyover crossing the A92 is reached and after this a tower, bounded by a wood, which, alas, is not visible from the road. This is Garden Tower, built in the sixteenth century and called after the burn which flows into Loch Gelly. It was here in 1826 that the last duel in Scotland was fought.

Carry on to the T-junction, turn right and follow this road to the next junction, then turn left and retrace this route back to Auchtertool.

At the junction with the B925 turn right, and then take the next junction on the left signposted for Puddledup. Go along this minor road between farms to the B9157 and turn left. After 4 km turn right on to the minor road signposted for Kinghorn, and take this route back there.

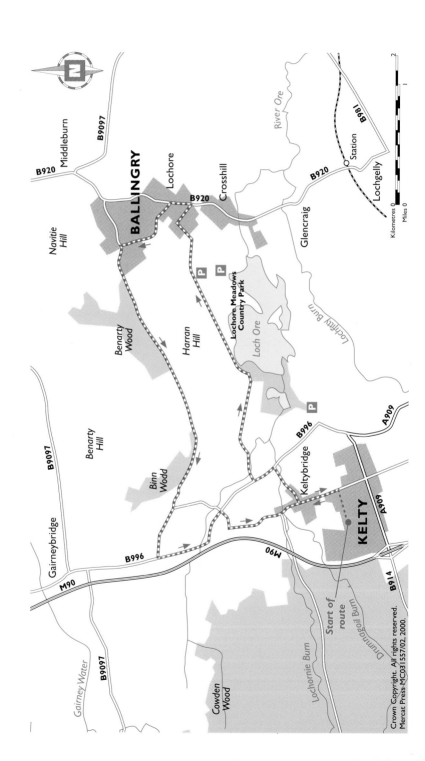

# KELTY TO BALLINGRY

Leave the car park and turn left on to Keltyhill Road and then turn left again on to Main Street (B917). Carry on along this street for a short distance and then fork to the right on to Black Road, still the B917, and head out of town. At the T-junction with the B996 turn left and follow this road for 200 m or so to a junction with a minor road. This is signposted for Lochore Meadows Country Park, where, as the signs will tell you, there is plenty to see and do—fishing, sailing, canoeing, windsurfing, rowing, horse-riding, golf, putting, bird-watching and much more besides. This park was formed from reclaimed coal-mining wasteland and is an excellent example of how to turn a blot on the landscape into an excellent public amenity. Carry on along the Pit Road as it runs parallel to the northern banks of Loch Ore. Soon the winding wheel of Mary Pit is reached, with a National Coal Board Tank Steam Engine standing next to it. These relics are kept as a monument to the noble industry which was so instrumental in giving Fife its prosperity, and, sadly, has all but vanished in this modern world.

## INFORMATION

**Distance:** 17 km (10.6 miles) circular route.

**Map:** OS Landranger, sheet 59; Kingdom of Fife Cycle Ways Kingdom Route map.

**Start and finish:** The car park on Keltyhill Road, Kelty.

**Terrain:** Generally fairly flat, with one prolonged hill through Ballingry.

**Refreshments:** Available in Kelty and at the tearoom in Lochore Meadows Country Park Visitors Centre.

Winding wheel of Mary Pit, Loch Ore Country Park.

From here, through the gate beside the winding wheel, is the path which leads to the Park Visitor Centre, which as well as many other facilities has a café. To the south of the Visitor Centre there can

be seen the ruins of Lochore Castle. A castle has existed here since 1255 and would have been in the form of a motte with a timber residence. The later stone castle was built on top of the motte around the end of the fourteenth century. This castle was lived in by a succession of prominent families in the area until the end of the seventeenth century. The castle would have stood on an island on the loch, which was partially drained in the 1790s. Once you have fully explored the

Cyclists visit Lochore Meadows Country Park.

park, return to Pit Road and continue in an easterly direction towards Lochore. Enter the town at Mannering Street and then turn right into Abbotsford Street, at the end of which turn left on to Lochleven Road. From here take the second road on the left, which is Ballingry Road, and carry on along this, climbing steadily, to its end at Hill Road. Turn left here and follow this road out of town. Continue to climb steadily for 600 m or so, at which point the road levels off for a short distance before beginning its long descent alongside Benarty Hill towards the B996 some 4 km further on.

On the right-hand side of this road, three-quarters of the way towards the junction with the B966, look out for the old stone bridge which was part of the ancient way from the Firth of Forth to St Johnstone (the old name for Perth). On its walls there are inscriptions, which were placed upon the bridge by William Adam, Chief Commissioner, in 1838. Over time the letters of these have almost been obliterated by the weather and are now nearly impossible to decipher. However, the bridge has been renovated recently and etched plaques on the bridge now relate what is in the inscriptions, as follows:

About this time 1) The Earl of Rothes with certain gentlemen came to Parenwell beside Downhill thinking to have taken my Lord Darnley from the Queen as they rode from St Johnstone to the Queensbury. But she being advertised [forewarned] had passed by before they met. 2) The road to Perth anciently called St Johnstone passed here within memory. The ravine was much longer and deeper, Cotter houses stood around called Parenwell from the spring that was a hundred yards below southward.

The first plaque probably refers to Andrew Leslie, 4th Earl of Rothes. It appears that he, and a group of gentlemen who were determined to do away with Lord Darnley, Mary Queen of Scots' first husband, made an attempt to capture him, against the Queen's will, at this spot. Obviously the Queen had been given information about this conspiracy and had passed before the conspirators arrived. However, there is no record elsewhere of this attempt actually having taken place. Nevertheless, it is possible that the Earl of Rothes may have had a part to play in the eventual assassination of Lord Darnley at Kirk o' Field in February 1567. Shortly after this event the Queen would certainly have passed this way on her way to imprisonment in Loch Leven Castle in June of the same year.

The old stone bridge over the Great North Road.

Go on again to the T-junction with the B966, turn right and head along this road for a kilometre to a junction on the right. Take this right turn along the minor road through the quaint little village of Maryburgh, followed by the equally quaint little village of Keltybridge. Continue on through Keltybridge to the junction with the B917 and then into Kelty. Head along Main Street and then turn right into Keltyhill Road and proceed back to the car park.

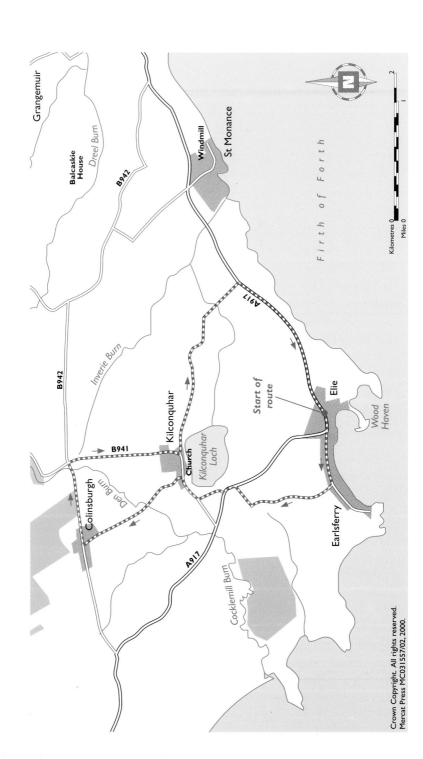

# ELIE AND EARLSFERRY TO COLINSBURGH

The once separate settlements of Elie, Liberty, Williamsburgh and Earlsferry were united as the burgh of Elie and Earlsferry in 1929. The burgh stretches for a mile around the bay from Sauchter Point to Kincraig Point.

Elie was created a Burgh of Barony in 1599, and at this time the harbour was built. This gave it the impetus to develop as an important centre of commerce, boat-building and fishing. At this time, too, weaving became an important local industry.

With the advent of the railway in the middle of the nineteenth century, Elie became a popular holiday resort, primarily for the middle classes, and unlike many other resorts all over Scotland it has retained its popularity. It is now a haven for yachts and small craft, and is one of few harbours in Scotland to be run by a private company on behalf of the people of the burgh. Elie has two golf courses and is also a centre for bowling, tennis, sailing and windsurfing.

Elie has many interesting buildings that span the centuries. One of them is the parish church, which

## INFORMATION

**Distance:** 15 km (9.4 miles) circular route.

**Map:** OS Landranger, sheet 59; Kingdom of Fife Cycle Ways East Neuk map.

**Start and finish:** The route begins in High Street where there are plenty of car parking places.

**Terrain:** A flat short route ideal for all the family.

**Refreshments:** Available in Elie, Kilconquhar and Colinsburgh.

Rough seas off the coast of Elie.

was built by Sir William Scott of Ardross in the 1630s. To the east, overlooking Ruby Bay, stand the ruins of The Lady's Tower, built as a seaside summer house for Janet Fall, Lady Anstruther. The remains of a hospice for pilgrims to St Andrews run by Cistercian nuns is situated at the rear of the town.

The famous golfer James Braid, who won the Open Championship five times between 1901 and 1910, was born in Elie. There is a plaque commemorating him on the front of the parish church. There is also a plaque presented by Polish Paratroops to the Royal Burgh of Elie and Earlsferry as a token of friendship and gratitude. They were stationed here between 1940 and 1943 during the Second World War.

The Royal Burgh of Earlsferry, situated west of Elie, is much older than its eastern neighbour. It was confirmed as a Royal Burgh by James VI in 1589, although there has been a royal tie since the reign of Alexander II in the thirteenth century. Earlsferry takes its name from the ferries that used to arrive here from North Berwick and Dirleton on

the Lothian coast, and their connection with the legend of Macduff, the Thane or Earl of Fife, who had a castle close by. He is said to have taken refuge from Macbeth in a cave at Kincraig point, while awaiting a ferry to take him across the Firth of Forth.

Kilconquhar Old Parish Church.

Start off along High Street in a westerly direction towards Earlsferry. Where the A917 turns right and inland, carry straight on to Bank Street and past the parish church. Follow this street through a number of name changes and then turn right into Ferry Road where it is signposted to Leven.

Carry on out of the village along this quiet little road which winds through gentle countryside. At the junction of the A917 turn left, and within a very short distance turn right again on to the B941, signposted for Cupar. Carry on for a kilometre into Kilconquhar, with a fine view of Kilconquhar Loch on the right. Opposite the fine old parish church at the Kinneuchar Inn turn left and head towards Colinsburgh. After passing the Equestrian Centre enter the small village of Colinsburgh, a planned village in the East Neuk of Fife built in 1705 for disbanded soldiers by Colin, 3rd Earl of Balcarres (1652–1722).

The Kinneuchar Inn, Kilconquhar.

Colinsburgh has a Town Hall dating from 1895 and the Galloway Library built in 1903. To the north lies Balcarres House, whose L-plan tower house was built in 1595 by the Lindsay family and later extended in the nineteenth century by the architects William Burn and David Bryce.

Turn right on to the B942. Soon the route passes the gates of Balcarres House and Chapel. Carry on a little further to the four-way junction, turn right and head back to Kilconquhar, passing *en route* Kilconquhar Estate. On entering Kilconquhar turn left into Balbouthie Road, following the signs for St Monance. Head uphill now for a short distance keeping close to Kilconquhar Loch. Carry on along this road for a little less than 3 km to the junction with the A917 and turn right. Although this is a main 'A' road which can be seasonally busy, it generally does not have the volume of traffic normally associated with such roads and should not cause any problems whilst cycling on it. However, be ever vigilant. Carry on along this road for 2 km back into High Street, Elie.

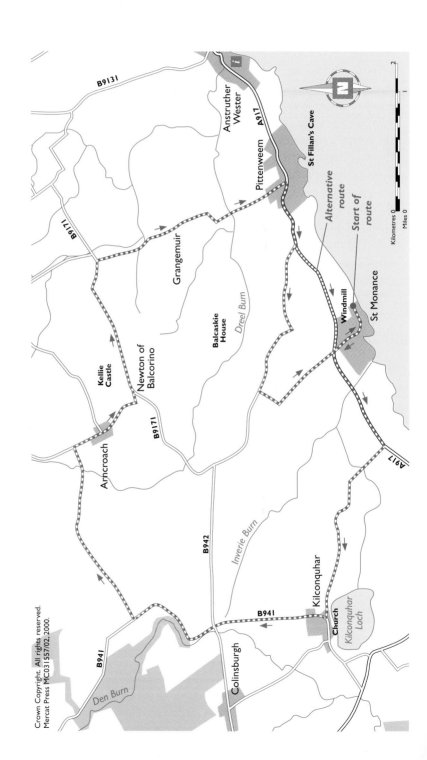

# ST MONANCE TO PITTENWEEM

S t Monance, like Pittenweem, Anstruther and Crail, is an ancient village full of interesting architecture and heritage. For many hundreds of years, as well as fishing, the locals built boats, mined coal and manufactured salt from local salt pans. There are two principal places of interest in St Monance. The first is the old church, which stands dramatically on the shore to the west of the village. It was dedicated to St Monance and founded by King David II in 1362, and transferred into the trust of the Dominican monks of St Andrews by James III, one hundred years later. After the Reformation it became derelict and by the end of the eighteenth century had been reduced to a ruin, although there were rumours that the church was a convenient place to hide smuggled items from time to time. Fortunately it was restored in the early nineteenth century by the architect William Burns and converted for use as a parish church, which it remains to this day. The second place of interest, lying to the east of the village, is the eighteenth-century windmill which has been recently refurbished.

The route begins at St Monance harbour. Proceed up Station Road, a reminder of the railway which once served this village, to the junction of the A917 and take this road in the direction of Elie for about a kilometre. This road, although sometimes busy, should not present much of a problem for most cyclists over this short distance. Take the first turning on the right which is the minor road signposted to Kilconquhar. Just before entering the village the road passes to the north of the splendid Kilconquhar Loch. Because this loch is fairly small it often freezes over in winter, and therefore it has become a popular place to hold a bonspiel (tournament) for those skilled in the game of curling. However, in the past it was said to have been used for a more sinister purpose—that of drowning

## INFORMATION

**Distance:** 20 km (12.5 miles) circular route.

**Map:** OS Landranger, sheet 59; Kingdom of Fife Cycle Ways East Neuk map.

**Start and finish:** At the harbour, St Monance.

**Terrain:** Generally flat with some short stretches of undulating road. Easy cycling for all the family.

**Refreshments:** Available from many places in St Monance and Pittenweem.

Old windmill at St Monance.

witches. This beautiful village with its eighteenth-century houses is worth stopping in for a look around.

On entering the village, turn right on to the B941 and head north, past the Kilconquhar estate with its castle which was built by Sir John Bellenden. The estate was soon acquired by the Earls of Lindsay, who later became the Earls of Crawford. This estate is now a premier holiday resort. Soon the junction with the B942 is reached. Carry straight on over this, continuing on the B941 signposted for St Andrews and Cupar. After a kilometre turn to the right and follow the minor road to Arncroach, turning to the right just before the village is reached. Carry on through Arncroach to the junction with the B9171 and turn left. Keep on this road for 1 km to where a minor road, signposted to Pittenweem, is to be found on the right, and follow this road straight into the village. Here there is a good view over the Firth of Forth with the Isle of May in the foreground.

View over Pittenweem Harbour.

Pittenweem is now the largest fishing port in the area, and if you are lucky enough to arrive when the fish sales are in progress, although I warn you that this will be very early in the morning, you will see a still-vibrant industry hard at work. This is not only an interesting spectacle, but it may give you the opportunity to buy some really fresh fish.

Pittenweem is as old as the other villages within the East Neuk and has links with St Fillan, another of the many seventh-century missionary saints to visit this part of the country. He is said to have worshipped in a cave which is situated in what is now Cove Wynd. This cave, with its 'saint well' and altar, was restored in 1935 and is still open to visitors today.

History has not always been kind or just to the people of Pittenweem, for in 1704 the infamous Pittenweem Witch Trials took place. The charges of witchcraft which led to these trials, and the shameful events that occurred as a result, were founded on the word of one man, Patrick Morton, the son of the local blacksmith. It happened because of an argument he had with Mrs Beatrix Laing, a woman of the village, about the making of some nails. In the weeks after this argument Morton became sick and concluded that Mrs Laing had put a spell on him. He publicly accused her and her neighbours, Thomas Brown and Janet Corphat, of using witchcraft against him. Morton claimed that the Devil had appeared to him and urged him to deny the name of his Saviour. On the insistence of the local minister, Mrs Laing was thrown into the town jail and under torture testified against her neighbours, but later retracted this testimony. The burgh authorities accepted her story and she was released. However, she was considered to be accursed by the locals and so she was banished from the community and lived out her life in St Andrews.

Pittenweem Priory.

The other accused were not so lucky. Thomas Brown was starved to death in Pittenweem prison and Janet Corphat became the victim of the mob who, incited by the minister, broke into the prison and seized her. They beat her and then crushed her to death by piling rocks on top of her.

On leaving the village one can either travel the two kilometres back to St Monance along the A917 or take the first road on the right after 200 m or so, which is the B942. Proceed along this to the junction at Abercromby and turn left on to the minor road leading back to St Monance and the finish of the route.

Caught napping—a young visitor to Pittenweem!

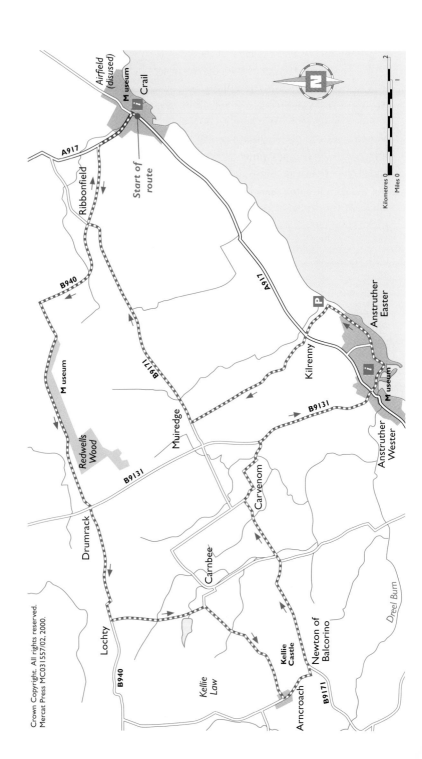

# CRAIL TO ANSTRUTHER

The route begins in High Street, Crail. Follow the A917 out of the village towards St Andrews. Soon the village gives way to rolling countryside on one side and a rugged coastline on the other. But this is an inland cycle route, and after only a few hundred metres you take the B940, signposted for Peat Inn and Cupar, and head gradually uphill away from the coast. At the crossroads of the B9171 carry straight on across the junction, continuing along this very quiet, flat, cycle-friendly road. After almost 6 km the entrance to the Secret Bunker is reached which is open to the public from April to the end of October.

The Secret Bunker was intended to be the underground nuclear command headquarters for Scotland and remained top secret until 1993. As you enter the bunker from the innocent-looking farmhouse that conceals it, through its hermetically sealed, blastproof doors, you begin to imagine what would have been happening in the outside world if it had ever had to be used.

Once back on the route you soon reach the junction with the B9131. Here turn right and immediately turn left again, once more keeping to the B940.

This flat road continues to where, at 10 km, a minor road signposted to Carnbee is located on the left. Take this slightly undulating road along which there are, on a clear day, wonderful views over the Firth of Forth. It was close to this point, in November 1918, that 49 ships of the Imperial German Navy began their journey into the Firth of Forth, flanked on either side by 180 ships of the British Grand Fleet with guns at the ready, stretching out all the way to the Forth Bridge. At the Forth Bridge they ceremoniously hauled down their flags before being escorted to Scapa Flow in Orkney to be interned. This internment ended suddenly on 21 June 1919 when the entire fleet was scuttled by its

## INFORMATION

**Distance:** 31 km (19.4 miles) circular route.

**Map:** OS Landranger, sheet 59; Kingdom of Fife Cycle Ways East Neuk map.

**Start and finish:** Crail—Car park on High Street or at the south end of West Green.

**Terrain:** Generally flat with a few short and gradual hills. Easy cycling for all the family.

**Refreshments:** Available from many places in Crail and Anstruther.

Lobster creels, Crail Harbour.

crews, in a gesture of defiance and protest at the severe conditions of the armistice.

After passing a small reservoir, with a fine view over to Kellie Law, you come to a T-junction. At this point turn right and follow the road past the back of Kellie Castle to Arncroach at 11½ km. Here turn left and continue on the road to where it joins the B9171 and turn left. Within a hundred metres of joining this road you will find the entrance to Kellie Castle.

The building of Kellie Castle was begun by the Oliphant family in the sixteenth century. It was then taken over by the Erskine family, who were created the Earls of Kellie in 1619. The castle was bought in the nineteenth century by the Lorimer family, and it was under Professor James Lorimer and his son Robert, the famous

Kellie Castle.

architect, that the beautiful restoration work, the results of which can be seen today, was carried out. The walled garden of the castle is also very charming and beautiful.

Sundial in the gardens at Kellie Castle.

After returning to the route from the castle turn left back on to the B9171, and continue for 3 km to where a minor road is seen on the right signposted for Anstruther. Turn here and go down this road until it joins the B9131. Turn right on to the B9131 and follow it into Anstruther, taking care when crossing over the A917.

Anstruther is made up of several communities dedicated to fishing, whose origins go back into antiquity. As with all the fishing villages along the East Neuk coast, Anstruther is a very beautiful place with its traditional architecture and narrow streets. As one would expect, it is dominated by the harbour which reflects its one-time status as one of the biggest fishing communities in the area. A new outer wall was constructed in the 1860s and the engineer in charge of the project was Thomas Stevenson, the father of one of Scotland's most famous writers, Robert Louis Stevenson. Robert stayed as a young man with his family at Cunzie House whilst this project was being carried out.

The village is the home of the Scottish Fisheries Museum in East Shore, which is well worth a visit.

Leave Anstruther by the following route. Go east along East Shore and at the edge of the harbour turn left, then right into James Street. Follow this street into the adjoining village of Cellardyke, where the street's name changes first to John Street and then to George Street, and as the harbour is reached it changes yet again to Shore Street. At the edge of the village, close to a carpark, a rough road climbs up to higher ground. Take this road as it carries on along the top of the slope adjacent to the coast. The road, much improved from this point, then turns inland, and soon the signalled junction with the A917 is reached. Continue straight across this junction into Kilrenny.

Gable end decorated with seashells, Anstruther.

Kilrenny is a quiet little village set back from the coast, with views overlooking the Forth. Kilrenny Parish Church was built in the fifteenth century, but only the tower remains from that date. The village has many eighteenth-century houses, the most interesting of which is Browlea Cottage in Trades Street, where the gable end follows the bend in the street.

After passing through this small attractive village continue along the minor road for 2½ km to the junction with B9171 again. Here turn right and carry on to the junction of the B940, at which point you should turn right and retrace the route back to Crail.

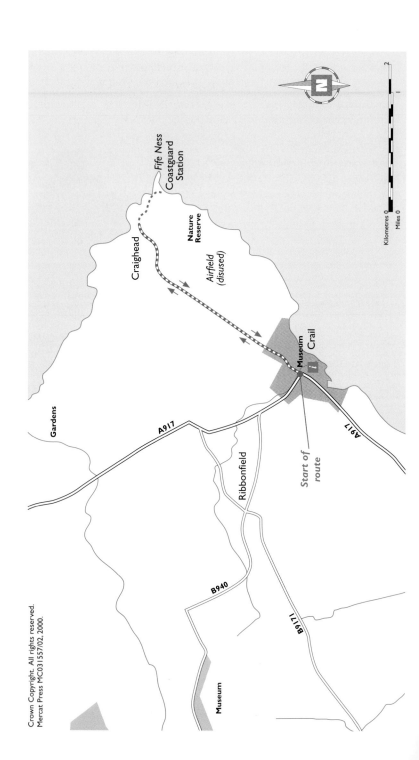

# CRAIL TO FIFE NESS

Crail is undoubtedly one of the most beautiful and historic villages in Scotland. A castle once existed here which was occupied from time to time by King David I, but no trace of it now remains. Crail was declared a Royal Burgh by King Malcolm IV in 1178. The village today is a maze of charming streets which radiate from the jewel in its crown—its picturesque harbour. This harbour once supported a substantial fishing fleet, but today there are only a few vessels remaining and they are confined to fishing for shellfish. From Crail Harbour can be seen the Isle of May, with its warning beacon. The Isle has a long history, for it was here in the ninth century that the missionary St Adrian was killed by marauding Danes. It is also a breeding ground for various kinds of sea-birds, guillemots and puffins in particular.

Crail Parish Church was built in the second half of the twelfth century, probably at the behest of King David I. It became a Collegiate church in 1517, and John Knox preached here in 1559. The celebrated

## INFORMATION

**Distance:** 8 km (5 miles) linear route.

**Map:** OS Landranger, sheet 59: Kingdom of Fife Cycle Ways East Neuk map.

**Start and finish:** Crail—Car park on the High Street or at the south end of West Green.

**Terrain:** Short and flat—easy cycling for all the family.

**Refreshments:** Available in Crail.

Crail Harbour.

James Sharp, Archbishop of St Andrews, was minister of the church in 1649, and his handwriting is still to be seen in the session records.

Crail Museum and Heritage Centre is located in Marketgate and has a fine exhibition of local history and tourist information.

The ghostly outline of the Isle of May.

Leave the village by heading northeast along Marketgate, and soon you will pass the now disused airfield on the outskirts of the village. It was known as HMS Jackdaw and was part of the Fleet Air Arm. During the Second World War it housed Swordfish planes with which naval crews practised torpedo-attack techniques. In the grounds of the airfield is Calminning Castle, a ruined medieval keep.

Balcomie Castle can be seen to the left of the road. It was built in the sixteenth century by the Learmouth family. Sir James Learmouth welcomed Mary of Guise, Mother of Mary, Queen of Scots, there in 1538, on her arrival from France. Part of this castle is still lived in today.

As the road heads eastward towards Fife Ness, the North Sea can be seen on either side of the road. After about 3 km, the golf course and the end of the road is reached. However, on the right just before the golf course, there is a small road leading to the Coastguard Station. Take this road and after about 500 m the gates to the Coastguard Station are reached. As one would expect, there is strictly no admittance to the station. However, from here there is a good view of the rocky coast and the North Sea beyond as far as St Abb's Head. Here too is the site of Fifeness Harbour. The harbour was first mentioned in 1537 as a customs area.

It was later used for bringing in stone. Also here is the great lighthouse, built, in the early part of the nineteenth century, by Robert Stevenson to his own design.

In 1807, Stevenson became the Lighthouse Commission's Chief Engineer. This was the same year he began work on the Bell Rock Lighthouse, the very first of his own design, and completed on its isolated rock in 1811. During Stevenson's service with the Commission, 23 lights were erected, many of them becoming of crucial importance for Scotland's maritime and strategic safety.

During the First World War, despite the Royal Navy's constant patrols of the area, German U-boats managed, fairly regularly, to breach the defences and get into the Firth of Forth, causing havoc to allied shipping. However, two of them, the U-12 and U-63, were sunk off the Isle of May. The U-63 was attacked by two British armed trawlers on 20 January 1918. She is lying in 52 m of water about 10 km south-east of the island. The U-12 lies a couple of miles further out.

In the Second World War, U-boats enjoyed even more success, with many Allied ships being torpedoed by them. Two steamships, the British *Avondale Park* and the Norwegian ship *Sneland 1* were particularly unlucky. They were both torpedoed by a U-boat one and a half miles off the Isle of May on 6 May 1945, at 11 am—one hour before the end of the war.

Sunset over Crail Bay.

This area is also a nature reserve, where a large variety of sea birds and water fowl can be seen. After investigating this interesting area thoroughly, simply turn and retrace the short route back to Crail.

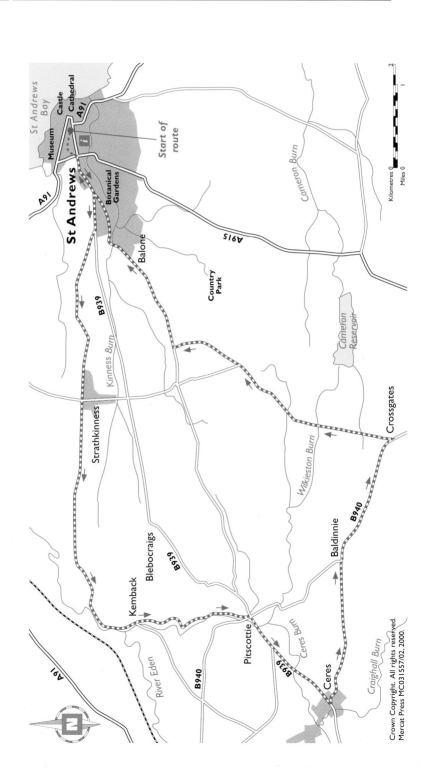

# ST ANDREWS TO CERES

St Andrews was created a burgh by King David I in 1144. The earliest records indicate that there has been a church on the site of St Andrew's Cathedral since the eighth century, and the eleventh-century St Rule's Tower is still partially standing. St Rule was believed to have brought relics of St Andrew here in the eighth century. This is when devotion to St Andrew began to take root, which eventually led to his adoption as Scotland's patron saint. It was said that he was crucified on a diagonal cross, and this is the origin of Scotland's national flag, the white saltire on a blue background.

The cathedral church, founded in the mid-twelfth century, was one of the largest in Britain. It was the principal cathedral of Scotland and, after 1472, seat of its first archbishop. The cathedral interior was destroyed by Protestant fanatics during the Reformation, but its present ruined condition is still awe-inspiring. The Cathedral Museum contains an important collection of early Christian sculptured stones. The most interesting item is the so-called sarcophagus of St Andrew, made to house the relics of Scotland's patron saint in either the eighth, or more probably the tenth, century.

St Andrew's Castle, now in ruins, was the residence of the bishops and archbishops of St Andrews from when it was built in about 1200, until the Reformation. During the Wars of Independence it changed hands several times between the Scots and the English, and sustained considerable damage on each occasion. It was rebuilt several times.

In 1546 Protestant rebels captured and killed Cardinal David Beaton and hung his corpse from the battlements of his own castle, in retaliation for his part in the burning of George Wishart, which had taken place in front of the building. The rebels,

## INFORMATION

**Distance:** 30 km (18.7 miles) circular route.

**Map:** OS Landranger, sheet 59; Kingdom of Fife Cycle Ways East Neuk map.

**Start and finish:** Tourist Information Centre in Market Street. Make your way to it from one of the many car parks within the town, as there is no railway into St Andrews.

**Terrain:** For most of the way this route follows sections of the Kingdom of Fife Cycle Network. Generally it is an undulating route with short stretches of steeper hills.

**Refreshments:** Available in St Andrews and Ceres.

St Andrews Cathedral.

St Andrews Castle.

joined by John Knox, then occupied the castle for a year until forced to surrender to besieging forces assisted by a French fleet. Knox and his fellows then spent two years serving on French galleys.

These are just a few of the interesting historical places to be seen in St Andrews. It is impossible to write about all of them here as there is so much to see. However, the reader would be well advised, before starting this cycle route, to spend some time exploring places such as the Church of St Mary's on the Rock, the University of St Andrews (the oldest university in Scotland, dating from 1412) and the oldest of its many colleges, the College of St Salvator (built in 1450)—to name but a few.

Golf has been played on the Links at St Andrews since around 1400 AD and the Old Course is re-nowned throughout the world as the Home of Golf.

The Royal and Ancient Golf Club, St Andrews.

All the golf courses at St Andrews Links are public—open to the golfers of the world. There are five 18-hole courses and one 9-hole course. The game was banned in 1457 by King James II of Scotland who felt it was distracting young men from archery practice. This ban was repeated by succeeding monarchs until James IV became a golfer himself in 1502.

The route begins at the Tourist Information Centre in Market Street. Follow the one-way-street system to Strathkinness High Road. Leave Market Street, turn left into Church Street and then right into South Street. After two blocks turn right into Bell Street and then left along St Mary's Place to the roundabout, at which point carry straight on into Doubledykes Road which becomes Hepburn Gardens. Continue along here for three blocks to a Y-junction and take the right fork into Buchanan Gardens. Soon another Y-junction is reached at which you turn right.

After 300 m or so the road starts to climb and soon

the city is left behind. Once in the countryside there is a good view over to Tentsmuir forest, the nature reserve on the mouth of the River Eden, and to St Andrews Bay. The road ascends gently for almost 4 km to Strathkinness. Cross a four-way junction and carry straight on to the Kemback Road. After 10 km a road junction is reached, and although the road to Kemback is off to the right, make a brief deviation to the left across the bridge to have a look at Dairsie Kirk in Dairsie Mains, with Dairsie Castle next to it. The interesting Gothic Kirk was built in 1621. The Castle, built in the sixteenth century as the home of the bishops and archbishops of St Andrews, was once a ruin, but has recently been rebuilt to reflect its former glory and is now a private residence.

Once returned to the route, within a short distance you reach a kind of natural grotto by the side of the road, where a seat has been placed by the Bahai International Community of East Fife.

After passing Kemback the road starts to climb towards Pitscottie. Turn left and almost immediately a four-way junction is reached. Turn right here and follow the signs for Ceres.

Once in Ceres it is time to look around again, for this village has much to interest the visitor. The climb out of Ceres on the minor road signposted for Peat Inn is quite steep at times to Baldinnie, at which point join the B949 and follow this road for almost 3 km to Crossgates. There turn right on to a minor road which is signposted to Strathkinness.

At Denhead take the road to the right and then a kilometre further on turn right at the T-junction towards St Andrews. Soon the entrance of Craigtown Country Park is reached. Carry on into St Andrews, entering the city once again at Hepburn Gardens. Now retrace the route through Doubledykes Road, across the roundabout into St Mary's Place and on into Market Street.

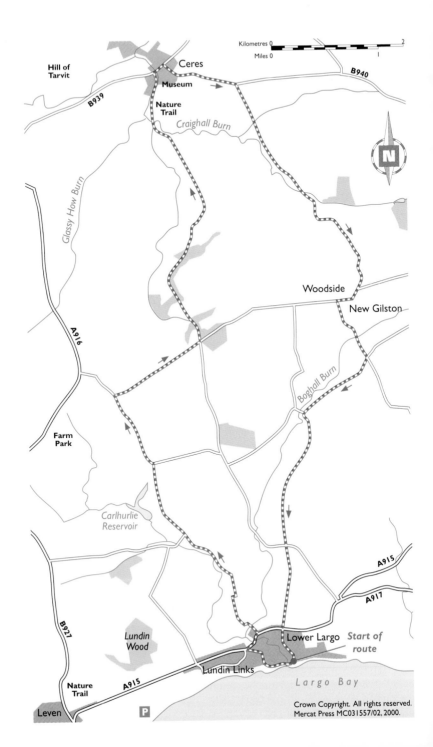

Kilometres 0 — 2
Miles 0 — 1

Hill of
Tarvit

B939

Ceres

B940

Museum

Nature
Trail

*Craighall Burn*

N

*Glassy How Burn*

A916

Woodside

New Gilston

*Boghall Burn*

Farm
Park

Carlhurlie
Reservoir

A915

A917

B927

*Lundin
Wood*

Lower Largo   *Start of
route*

Lundin Links

*Largo Bay*

Nature
Trail

A915

P

Leven

Crown Copyright. All rights reserved.
Mercat Press MC031557/02, 2000.

# CERES TO LOWER LARGO

Ceres was famous for its handloom weaving of linen, but, alas, that cottage industry has now all but died out. There is a small museum dedicated to the folk heritage of the area. On the way into Ceres from the east, one has to cross the Bishop's Bridge, which Archbishop James Sharp crossed in 1679 on his journey through Magus Muir, where he was dragged out of his carriage by a group of Covenanters and brutally murdered in front of his daughter, who had been travelling with him.

Turn right out of the car park and then turn right again on to St Andrew's Road, and on past the monument which commemorates the many men of Ceres who fought so valiantly at the Battle of Bannockburn in 1314. This was the battle which sealed Scotland's independence from England and put Robert the Bruce on the Scottish throne.

Carry on through the centre of the village and then turn right onto the Anstruther Road. This road also becomes the Kingdom of Fife Cycle Route, signposted for Peat Inn. The climb out of Ceres is quite steep at times.

INFORMATION

**Distance:** 24 km (15 miles) circular route.

**Map:** OS Landranger, sheet 59; Kingdom of Fife Cycle Ways Howe of Fife East map.

**Start and finish:** The Folk Museum car park off Teasses Road, Ceres.

**Terrain:** Undulating with prolonged stretches of steep hills.

**Refreshments:** Available in Ceres and Lower and Upper Largo. Of particular note is 'The Scottish Larder' situated at the north boundary of Upper Largo on the A917.

Carry on along this road for a kilometre to where the cycle route is signposted to Peat Inn and turn right. Follow this minor road as it rises and falls through in-

Birds cluster in the fields at Ceres.

teresting landscapes for 3 km to a T-junction. As this stretch of road passes through several farmyards it is rough and uneven in places, so take care. Turn right at the T-junction, away from the cycle route, continue for less than 200 m and turn left. The route once again starts to climb for about a kilometre to a four-way junction, at which turn right. Here you will see the first views of Largo Bay on the right and Largo Law on the left. The road soon starts its often steep descent towards sea level. After another kilometre bear left at the next junction.

The road, which now passes by the 290 m high Largo Law, descends, with the exception of one or two short uphill stretches, to a four-way junction, at which go straight ahead, on the road signposted to Lundin Links. Continue uphill quite steeply for a short distance before once again descending into Lower Largo.

Soon the junction with the A915 at the War Memorial is reached. Here cycle straight on into Harbour Wynd, which then becomes Station Wynd as it passes under the Railway Viaduct, and go on to the junction with Main Street. Turn left here into Lower Largo.

The memorial in Lower Largo to Andrew Selkirk, the original 'Robinson Crusoe'.

For centuries Lower Largo was a prosperous fishing village, noted for its manufacture of nets and knitwear. The famous eighteenth-century English writer Daniel Defoe visited Lower Largo in 1706, and was inspired to write *The Life and Surprising Adventures of Robinson Crusoe*, after visiting the birthplace of Alexander Selkirk and hearing his story. Selkirk, after quarrelling with fellow officers of his ship, the *Cinque Ports,* was marooned by them on one of the uninhabited islands in the Juan Fernandez group, 1,000 km due west of Santiago, Chile, in the Pacific Ocean, for four years. There is a statue commemorating 'Robinson Crusoe' on the site of the house where Selkirk was born in 1676, just a little further along Main Street.

The full name of the village is Seatown of Largo. There was a steamboat service from here to Newhaven on the south coast of the Firth of Forth during the nineteenth century, but this stopped once the railway was built. The railway which passed along this imposing viaduct was completed in 1856.

This made Lower Largo, with its fine sandy beach, a popular tourist centre, a reputation it enjoyed until well into the twentieth century. The village was designated a conservation area in 1978.

After a good look around this interesting village, retrace your way to the junction of Main Street and Station Wynd. From here the route carries straight on across the bridge over Keil Burn into Drummochy Road and uphill. At the top of the hill turn right into Emsdorf Road, then go straight on into Hillhead Street. At the end of this street turn left into Mill Wynd and within a short distance you come to the junction with Largo Road (A915). Here turn right on to this busy road and proceed uphill, but only for about 100 m, before turning left at the road which is signposted for Cupar and called Hatton Road.

Once you are on this minor road, open country is soon reached. The road climbs consistently uphill for just over 4 km, with short stretches of steep incline and quite a few right-angle bends, to the junction signposted for New Gilston and Peat Inn. Here turn right and follow this road for 1½ km. Along this stretch of road you are rewarded for your efforts in getting here. For there is now a most spectacular 360-degree panoramic view which, on a clear day, must extend about a hundred miles. It stretches from the Breadalbane and Grampian mountains in the north, to the Firth of Forth and the Lothians beyond in the south, and to the Lomond Hills in the west.

Largo Law.

At the next four-way junction turn left on to the Ceres Road and continue uphill through a wooded area. Once through the wood the road then runs past picturesque fields and streams and on into Ceres, entering the village at Teasses Road. Here the car park where the route began is soon located.

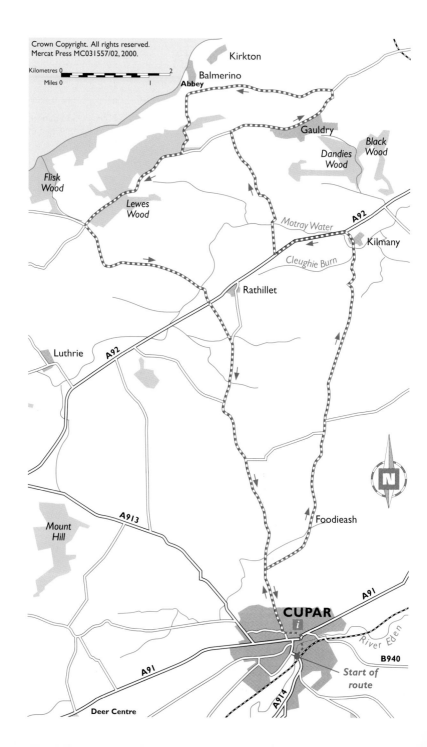

Kilometres 0         2
Miles 0         1

Kirkton

Balmerino
**Abbey**

Gauldry

*Black Wood*

*Dandies Wood*

*Flisk Wood*

*Lewes Wood*

Motray Water   A92

Kilmany

Cleughie Burn

Rathillet

Luthrie   A92

*Mount Hill*

A913

Foodieash

**CUPAR**
*i*

A91

River Eden

B940

*Start of route*

A91

A914

**Deer Centre**

# CUPAR TO BOTTOMCRAIG VIA THE GAULDRY

Leave the railway station and turn right into Station Road which itself turns through 90 degrees. Turn right once again into East Bridge and then immediately left into East Burnside. Carry straight on along this road and take the third junction on the right, which leads into North Burnside, following the signs for the hospital. Soon the boundary of the town and open country are reached. After 500 m or so take the right fork at the road junction signposted for Kilmany, Logie and Foodieash. Foodieash is the first place to be reached, after which the road starts its ascent, first alongside Foodie Hill and then by Forret Hill. There are some beautiful farmhouses dotted along this stretch of the route.

At the next junction carry straight on, ignoring the cycle sign for Wormit and Newport. Two kilometres further on the road descends steeply, with two 90-degree bends to negotiate, so take care. On now to Kilmany. After crossing the beautiful old bridge which spans Motray Water, the road turns east to reveal a statue of a young man who looks as if he is in a hurry. The young man is Jim Clark, the famous Formula One racing driver who was born in Kilmany in 1936. He had a natural driving talent which might have made him the greatest driver of all time, had his career not been cut short by a tragic accident in 1968 during a race at Germany's flat-out Hockenheim course. In almost nine years on the Formula One circuit, Clark had won 25 out of the 72 races he had entered, and was twice Formula One World Champion.

At the end of this small picturesque village the A92 is reached. Turn left here and carry on along this road for a little less than 1 km to where a road junction is signposted for Gauldry and Balmerino. Take this minor road, and after an initial, short

### INFORMATION

**Distance:** 32 km (20 miles) circular route.

**Map:** OS Landranger, sheet 59; Kingdom of Fife Cycle Ways Howe of Fife West map.

**Start and finish:** At Cupar Railway Station.

**Terrain:** Undulating with long stretches of sustained hills in places.

**Refreshments:** Available from many places in Cupar. Limited refreshments can also be had in Gauldry.

Young man in a hurry—the Jim Clark Memorial in Kilmany.

uphill stretch, the road winds downhill and underneath a disused railway before climbing steeply to Fincraigs. On now to a T-junction and turn right to Gauldry.

Enter 'The Gauldry', as it is known, where refreshments can be obtained. Tarry awhile in this pleasant little village before setting off again on your cycle tour. Gauldry once had its own small weaving industry and it was also the home of workers from the surrounding estates. However, today it is populated largely by people who work in Dundee or other nearby towns.

View across the River Tay.

Just on the outskirts of Gauldry there is a fine panorama of the River Tay with its two bridges, with a good view of Dundee on the far side as the road winds downhill. At the bottom of this hill a junction is reached. Turn left here once again, joining the Kingdom of Fife Cycle Routes to Newburgh and Auchtermuchty.

The house on the right is Naughton House, dating from 1793. It stands next to Naughton Castle, built in the sixteenth century by the Hay family who were related to the Earls of Errol.

Carry on along this road past Bottomcraig, a tiny hamlet with a fine old church, then turn right and head towards Kirkton of Balmerino, passing a glass-engraving studio on the way. Just before Balmerino, as you head towards the coast, there is a beautiful view across the Tay with the Perthshire hills behind. On entering Balmerino there is an interesting old cemetery on the left with some Jacobite graves.

After you pass through this picturesque little village, Balmerino Abbey is reached. This was built in 1229, on the instructions of Queen Ermengarde, widow of King William the Lion and a direct descendant of William the Conqueror, for Cistercian monks from Melrose. The location was chosen because of its sheltered position and healthy climate. When the Queen died in 1233, she was buried in front of the high altar. The original building was added to several times by the monks during its long and generally peaceful history. However, its tranquillity was disturbed on Christmas night in 1547, when an invading English force set the Abbey alight. The Abbey was soon repaired, only to be further damaged 12 years later by the Reformers, and now only the vaulted chapter house and a section of the cloisters remain. The Abbey is now in the care of the National Trust for Scotland.

Balmerino Abbey.

After leaving the Abbey carry on to a T-junction and turn right. In this stretch of the route there are short but steep hills to negotiate. After about a kilometre yet another T-junction is reached. Here, once again, the Kingdom of Fife Cycle Route is joined. This time turn right and follow the cycle sign, still in the direction of Newburgh and Auchtermuchty. The undulating road still winds uphill for a while to a four-way junction. Here turn left, away from the cycle route.

Soon the ruined castle of Mountquhanie can be seen on the right. This fifteenth-century castle was built by the Balfour family, who were very prominent in the area. Sir James Balfour was involved in the murder of Cardinal David Beaton in 1546. The castle went on to become the property of General Robert Lumsden, the Covenanter Governor of Dundee, who was killed defending the city against the forces of General Monk in 1651.

The ruined castle of Mountquhanie.

Carry straight on to the junction with A914 and cross this, continuing along the minor road signposted for Cupar. Follow this road for 6 km all the way back to Cupar.

Once back in Cupar the route ends as it began, so return the same way you came to Cupar Railway station.

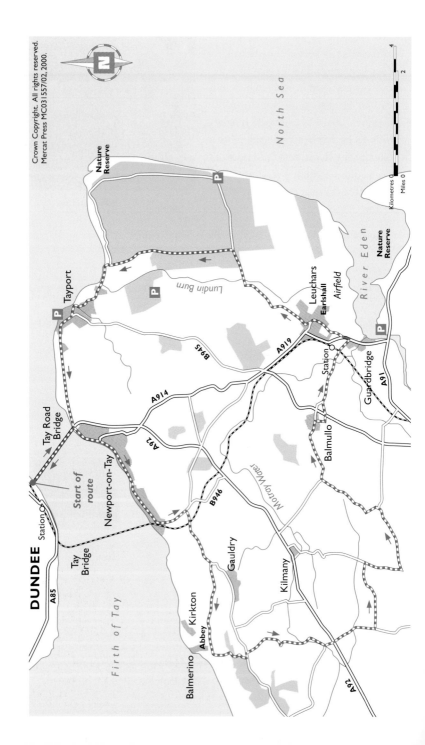

# DUNDEE TO LEUCHARS

L eave Dundee Railway Station and turn right. Cross Riverside Drive at the pedestrian crossing on to Discovery Quay where the *Discovery* is berthed. Follow the quay around past the side of the Olympia Leisure Centre and then on to the river edge, and soon the Tay Road Bridge is reached.

Construction of the Tay Road Bridge began in March 1963 and it took three and a half years to build. It was opened by Her Majesty the Queen Mother on 18 August 1966. At 2,250 m it had the longest river crossing of any road bridge in Britain, until the second Severn Bridge was opened in 1996, with a length of 5,168 m.

Follow the sign for the lift which takes pedestrians and cyclists on to the walkway and cycleway which runs along the middle of the bridge between the two carriageways. The experience of cycling across this bridge is a noisy one, although on a fine day the views are spectacular. Once on the Fife side go down the ramp and turn left into a car park. Continue to the exit of the car park, turn left and descend to the junction of the B946. Turn left and continue through Newport-on-Tay and then enter the village of Wormit. At the southern edge of the village turn right and follow the Kingdom of Fife cycle signs for Balmullo and Leuchars. Once on this minor road proceed uphill and just after a kilometre turn right to follow the cycle signs once again. Carry on past Bottomcraig and soon the road to Balmerino Abbey is reached. This has been described in Route 16. Once past this turning the road begins a sustained climb with very steep sections. At the top of this hill a junction is reached. Here turn left and almost immediately right on to another minor road signposted to 'The Grange'. This now begins a long descent. At the next junction turn left and soon the A92 is reached. Cross

### INFORMATION

**Distance:** 46 km (28.7 miles) circular route.

**Map:** OS Landranger, sheet 59; Kingdom of Fife Cycle Ways Howe of Fife East map.

**Start and finish:** Dundee Railway Station.

**Terrain:** Flat in parts, but generally undulating with some prolonged steep stretches. A picturesque rural route with plenty of scenery but not so much history.

**Refreshments:** Available in Dundee, Wormit, Leuchars, Tayport and Newport-on-Tay.

The *Discovery* at her berth in Dundee.

this road, with care, and go along it for about a kilometre, then turn left, still following the cycle signs. After 500 m head to the right. Follow this road for another 500 m to a T-junction and turn left at the sign for Kedlock and Feus and the cycle route.

View over St Andrews Bay.

The road carries on through a pleasant farmyard and on to the next junction, where a right turn is made. This road soon begins to descend steeply. After a kilometre turn left, still following the cycle signs. The road now begins to climb gradually at first and then much more steeply, as the Craigsanquhar Hotel is reached. After another kilometre you reach Logie. Soon after passing Logie Estate there is another junction. Carry straight on here, and from this high vantage point at Lucklaw you will have a beautiful view over the mouth of the Tay on one side and St Andrews Bay on the other. Carry on along this single-track road passing through a quarry and then wind down hill, carefully watching out for oncoming lorries, into Balmullo. Turn right on to School Road and then turn left along Lucklaw Road. Cross the A914 into Clay Road, following the cycle signs for Leuchars. After 2 km pass Milton Houses and then pass over the railway bridge and on to the junction with the A919. Here take the west footpath for about 50 m and then cross the A919, following the cycle signs for Leuchars and Tayport. Once on this road cycle past the RAF station into Leuchars. In Leuchars turn right into Pitlethie Road and follow the cycle signs for Tayport, passing the twelfth-century

Norman church *en route*. The church of St Athernase is said to be the finest Romanesque church in Scotland. It was built between 1183 and 1187 and dedicated by Bishop de Bernham in 1244. A new nave was added to the church in the nineteenth century. On Castle Knowe, behind the church, there once stood the castle of the De Quincy family who were the original builders of the church. However, no trace of this castle now remains.

Follow this narrow minor road for 2½ km to the junction, and following the signs for Kinshaldy Beach turn right into Tentsmuir Forest. After a little less than a kilometre there is a cycle sign which points the direct route to Tayport on the left. Take this forestry road, known as Ash Road, for 4 km, past the Meteorological Station, and on into Tayport via Shanwell Road South, Links Road North and Promenade.

Tayport is situated at the mouth of the Firth of Tay, and today is principally a dormitory town for Dundee and St Andrews. Known as Ferryport-on-Craig until 1846, it was, as the name suggests, for many centuries a ferry port linking Fife with Dundee and Broughty Ferry. The town was transformed in the nineteenth century, firstly by the arrival of the railway and the creation of a railway ferry in the 1840s, and secondly with the opening of the Tay Rail Bridge in 1878. In 1847 its harbour was rebuilt by Thomas Grainger for the Northern Railway Co. to accommodate paddle steamers.

Looking over the Tay Road Bridge to Dundee.

Above the village on Hare Law, to which one could cycle, there is a tower which commemorates the defeat of Napoleon at Waterloo in 1815.

Join the B948 and carry on to the access road for the Tay Bridge, retracing your original route back across the bridge to Dundee.

The cycle track over the Tay Road Bridge.

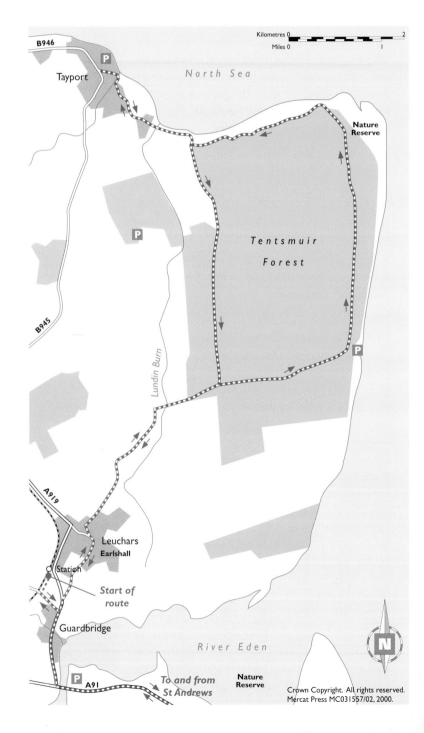

Kilometres 0 2
Miles 0 1

B946

Tayport

*North Sea*

P

**Nature Reserve**

P

*Tentsmuir Forest*

B945

*Lundin Burn*

P

A919

Leuchars
**Earlshall**

Station

*Start of route*

Guardbridge

*River Eden*

N

P A91

*To and from St Andrews*

**Nature Reserve**

Crown Copyright. All rights reserved.
Mercat Press MC031557/02, 2000.

# LEUCHARS TO TAYPORT

I f you decide to start the route from St Andrews, follow the busy A91 to Guardbridge. At points along this stretch you are permitted to use the footway, but only where you see the cycle signs. From Guardbridge follow the cycle signs as the route begins along the A919 towards Leuchars. There are short stretches of cycle route available, so get off the main road when you can. The route joins the Kingdom of Fife Cycle Network at Mottray Crescent on the outskirts of Leuchars. Just beyond there is Toll Road, at which point the Kingdom of Fife Cycle route is joined. It is signposted to Leuchars Station, where six cycle parking stands can be found.

Most of the area on which the present village of Leuchars is situated is land which was drained in the eighteenth century. At Castle Knowe, just to the north of the village, is where Leuchars Castle

### INFORMATION

**Distance:** 25 km (15.7 miles) circular route (with a further 18 km, 11.2 miles, if starting and finishing the route from St Andrews).

**Map:** OS Landranger, sheet 59; Kingdom of Fife Cycle Ways Howe of Fife East map.

**Start and finish:** Leuchars Railway Station.

**Terrain:** Relatively easy and flat, suitable for all the family.

**Refreshments:** Available in Leuchars and Tayport.

Leuchars Parish Church with its Romanesque tower.

once stood. There has also been a church here since the twelfth century, and the original Romanesque tower still forms part of Leuchars parish church. The village grew in prosperity when the railway was built in 1848, and then in 1917 the Royal Navy established an RNAS fleet fighter station, although Leuchars' association with aviation can be traced even further back to 1911 when military balloons were operated at the site. Later it became a Royal Air Force Coastal Command airfield. After the Second World War, Leuchars became a Fighter Command Station, and continues in this role today as one of the RAF's Air Defence bases.

Another place of historical importance in Leuchars is Earlshall Castle, situated along Earlshall Road. The main part of the Castle is still lived in, but there is a museum section open to the public. Construction of this castle was begun in 1546 by Sir William Bruce, and completed by his great-grandson William in 1617. However, the castle fell into disrepair and was only rescued in 1891 when Sir Robert Lorimer started to restore it, as he and his father had done at Kellie Castle.

Turn right out of Leuchars Station and proceed along a minor road to a T-junction. Turn left and follow this road, known as Toll Road, to the junction with the A919. Here take the west footpath of this main road for about 50 m and then cross the A919, following the cycle signs for Leuchars and Tayport into the Croft. Once on this road, cycle past the RAF station into Leuchars.

Once in Leuchars turn right into Pitlethie Road, following the cycle signs for Tayport, past the twelfth century Norman church (mentioned already in Route 17). Follow this narrow minor road for 2½ km to the junction, and following the signs for Kinshaldy Beach turn right. Continue along this road into Tentsmuir Forest as far as the car park and Kinshaldy picnic area. This forest, mainly

Members of the local cycling club out for a day by the sea.

Scots pine, has an abundant variety of fauna and flora, and together with the beautiful beaches on the coast along its edge, offers the visitor an interesting day out.

From this point continue along the track designated for cycling. It runs north, past Tentsmuir Sands, to the ice-house built in the last century to keep the salmon, caught in the Tay Estuary, fresh. Then it continues to Tentsmuir Point, where it turns west, parallel to the Tay Estuary, into Tayport via Shanwell Road South and Links Road North.

On the return journey retrace the route back to the end of Shanwell Road South, and at the Meteorological Station turn left along Ash Road which is signposted as Leuchars Direct Route. This track continues all the way back to Kinshaldy Beach Road, where you turn right and retrace the route back to Leuchars or St Andrews.

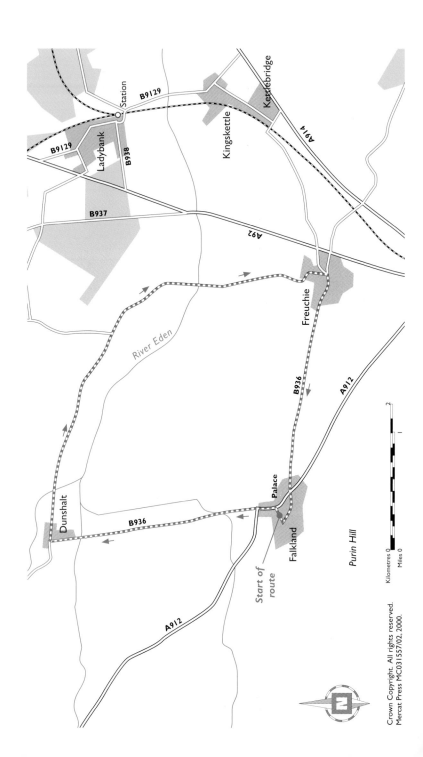

# FALKLAND TO FREUCHIE

Falkland, situated at the head of the Eden Valley, was, in the twelfth century, an area of great strategic importance, as it was located on the ancient north/south route. Therefore, it was here that Macduff, the Thane of Fife, had a castle built, from which he was able to control the surrounding area. Later, James III purchased the property, and in 1458 granted the town a Royal Charter.

Falkland Palace was built by James IV around 1500. It was the favourite hunting lodge of the Stuart kings and was used extensively by both James IV and James V. In fact the latter died here, ostensibly from a fever, but more likely of a broken heart after being defeated by his uncle, Henry VIII, at the battle of Solway Moss. Not even the news of the birth of his daughter Mary (the future Queen of Scots) could lighten his acute melancholy. James V had a catchpole (Royal tennis court) built for him in the palace in 1539. This ancient game was invented by the kings of France, and today there is still a thriving Royal Tennis Club here in Falkland. There are only a very few Royal tennis courts left in Britain, and the one in Falkand is the only one of its kind in the world.

## INFORMATION

**Distance:** 13 km (8.1 miles) circular route.

**Map:** OS Landranger, sheet 59; Kingdom of Fife Cycle Ways Howe of Fife West map.

**Start and finish:** Falkland—car park at Back Wynd.

**Terrain:** For most of the way the route follows sections of the Kingdom of Fife Cycle Network. Generally it is very flat, with short stretches of slightly undulating road. Easy even for the most inexperienced cyclist.

**Refreshments:** Available at many places in Falkland and Freuchie.

Traditional Scottish two-storey house, Falkland.

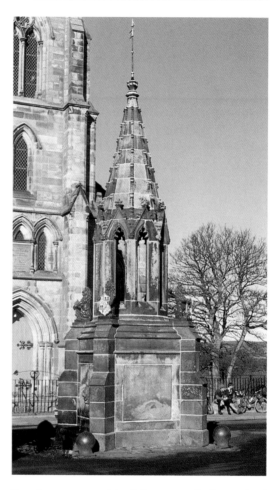

The Merkat Cross, Falkland.

Royal patronage of the Palace severely diminished after the Union of the Crowns, although Charles II did visit the palace on one occasion.

Much of the palace was destroyed by an accidental fire started by Cromwell's troops in 1653 whilst they were in occupation during the Civil War. It was extensively restored by John Patrick Stuart, the royal keeper of the palace, in 1887.

Falkland was once a centre for the textile and linoleum industries, but sadly these have now closed. It became the first Conservation Area in Scotland, and its main industry now is tourism.

Leave the car park and turn right on to Back Wynd and then turn right into Eastport. Cycle down Eastport for 150 m past the Palace to the junction with Pleasance. Turn left on to New Road and continue for 300 m to the junction of the B936, which is signposted for Dunshalt and Auchtermuchty, and turn right. This road forms part of the Kingdom of Fife Cycle Network, and this is signposted from this junction. Use the advisory cycle lanes provided to cycle along this stretch of flat road to Dunshalt some 3 km further on. Once Dunshalt has been reached, carry on through this very picturesque little village to a T-junction and turn right, away from the Kingdom of Fife Cycleway, on to the minor road signposted for Freuchie. Once on this quiet and flat minor road it is 8 km to Freuchie through the Howe of Fife.

Once Freuchie is reached, go along Unthank. This street with the strange-sounding name ends at the junction with Eden Valley Row. Turn right and follow this road to the junction with High Street and turn right again. Continue along High Street (B936) out of the village and on to Falkland, following the signs for the Kingdom of Fife Cycle Network once again. This time only the route is signed.

Cyclists taking a well-earned break in Falkland.

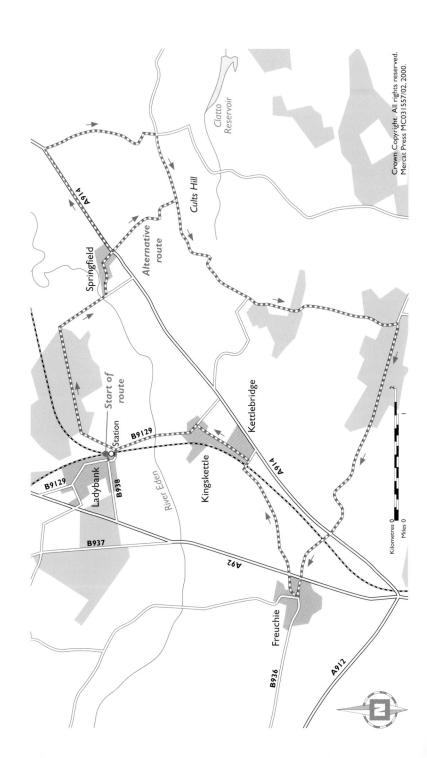

# FREUCHIE TO LADYBANK

Freuchie is only a short distance to the east of Falkland. It is said to have been first colonised by a group of French masons who, during the sixteenth century, were employed on the construction of one of the phases of Falkland Palace. Later it became a place of banishment for disgraced courtiers. This gave rise to the old saying: 'Awa tae Freuchie whair the Froggies bide'.

The route begins at the Merket Cross in Freuchie. Turn left and follow the Kingdom of Fife Cycle Route sign to Kingskettle and Ladybank. After about half a kilometre cross the busy A914 trunk road, taking great care.

Carry on along this flat minor road until a railway bridge is reached. After turning under this bridge, turn sharp left and continue along the road, known as Rumdewan, towards Kingskettle. Turn left into Main Street and go across two junctions into Ladybank Road.

This fertile farming area, known as the Howe of Fife, is almost at the centre of the Kingdom. It lies in the valley of the River Eden between Strathmiglo and Cupar. The term 'howe' is an old Scots word meaning a valley or flat expanse of land.

Kingskettle developed in the nineteenth century with the creation of the turnpike road at the start of the century and the opening of the railway to Cupar in 1847.

The MP for this area in the late nineteenth and early twentieth centuries was Herbert Henry Asquith. A Yorkshireman by birth, Asquith worked as a barrister until becoming Liberal MP for East Fife in

## INFORMATION

**Distance:** 19 km (12 miles) circular route.

**Map:** OS Landranger, sheet 59; Kingdom of Fife Cycle Ways Howe of Fife West map.

**Start and finish:** At the Lomond Hills Hotel.

**Terrain:** Flat along the Howe of Fife stretch, and then climbing, sometimes steeply, up to Cults Hill.

**Refreshments:** Available from a few inns along the route.

View of the Lomond Hills from the Howe of Fife.

1886. He was appointed Home Secretary by William Gladstone in 1892 and held the post successfully until the defeat of the Liberal government in 1905. He became prime minister when Sir Henry Campbell-Bannerman, a Glaswegian by birth, retired in 1908.

Asquith's government was responsible for introducing a series of social reforms between 1908 and 1914 including Old Age Pensions, National Health Insurance and National Unemployment Insurance. It was a period of some turmoil, with the activities of the suffragettes and the threat of civil war in Ireland. These conflicts, however, were as nothing in comparison to the outbreak of the Great War in 1914.

Once in Ladybank Road (B9129) carry straight on towards Ladybank. This flat road continues into Ladybank and soon comes to a junction. Go straight ahead here, following the sign for Springfield, on to Pitlessie Road. After 2 km a T-junction is reached. Turn right here and follow the minor road into Pitlessie. At this point cross the busy A92 with care.

Pitlessie is the birthplace of Sir David Wilkie, one of Scotland's most revered artists. He was born in 1785, in the manse of Cults Kirk, which is less than a kilometre away from Pittlessie in Kirkton of Cults. His father, also David, was the minister there. His first famous work, 'Pitlessie Fair', was painted at the manse in 1804 when Wilkie was only nineteen. This painting, now hanging in the National Gallery of Scotland, depicts the local cattle fair in the village. In 1823 Wilkie succeeded Sir Henry Raeburn as the King's Painter in Scotland, and was knighted in 1836.

At this point, depending on your prowess on a bicycle and your level of fitness, there are two alternative ways to continue. The first, for the more adventurous, is to take the unsignposted road straight ahead of you. This is an unsurfaced road, which is muddy and in some places severely rutted. However, as it only lasts for a kilometre, if it is too difficult to cycle in places it is easy enough to walk. The author was able to complete this stretch without having to dismount. Cycle along this road as it begins to climb, sometimes steeply, towards the top of Cults Hill, where it joins the cycle route for Star of Markinch and Glenrothes at a T-junction, and turn right.

The alternative route is to turn left at the junction with the A92 and carry on along this busy road for 1½ km. On this stretch there is an informal path by the side of the road that can be used. At the end of this short stretch turn right on to the minor road signposted for Cults Hill and Chance Inn. This road then climbs gradually for 1½ km to a four-way junction where you should turn right, following the cycle signs in the direction of Star and Glenrothes. Carry on along this road for a kilometre to where the first of these alternative routes joins from the right, and continue straight on.

The road becomes flatter now through Burnturk. After Burnturk climb a steep hill to another junction and carry straight on, still following the Star road. This road climbs steeply again for a short distance. At the next junction turn right, following the signs for Freuchie and Kingskettle. This wooded road continues, with the Lomond Hills now clearly visible some distance ahead. Then it begins to descend into the Howe of Fife. At the

Journey's end at the Lomond Hills Hotel, Freuchie.

next junction cross the A92 and take the 20 m long cycle track; then turn left to follow this minor road to the junction of the A914, carrying straight on into Freuchie and the end of the route at the Lomond Hills Hotel.

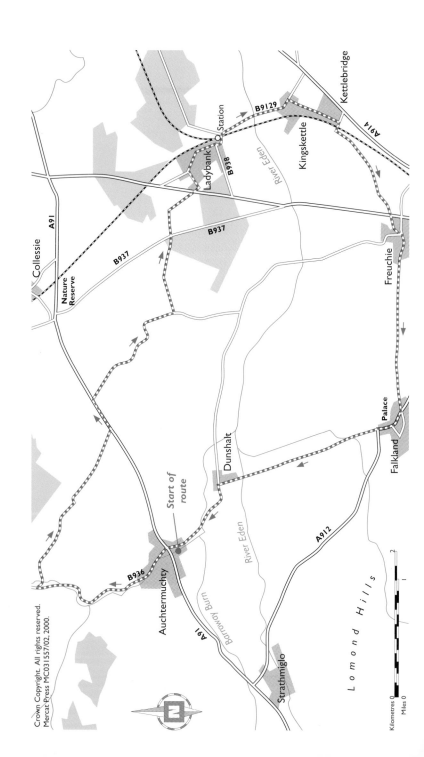

Kettlebridge

B9129

Station

Kingskettle

Ladybank

B938

A914

River Eden

Collessie

A91

B937

Freuchie

Nature Reserve

B937

Palace

Falkland

Dunshalt

River Eden

Start of route

A912

B936

Auchtermuchty

A91

Barnaway Burn

Strathmiglo

Lomond Hills

Kilometres 0    1    2

Miles 0    1

# AUCHTERMUCHTY TO LADYBANK

The name of Auchtermuchty, somewhat unusual and perhaps difficult to pronounce, depending on what part of the country you come from, is thought to mean 'the high ground of the wild boar'. This is because in medieval times the large oak forest which used to surround the village was the home to many species of wild animals, including wild boar, and therefore became a favourite hunting ground of the kings and earls of Scotland. Auchtermuchty was granted a Royal Charter in 1517 by King James V. Its oldest house, standing on the west side of the town square, is Macduff House, which was the home of the Earls of Fife.

There is a famous folktale about the people of Auchtermuchty. Once, many centuries ago, the good people of the town were so devout in their religious beliefs that they managed to anger the Devil. So he came amongst them in the guise of a Presbyterian minister in the hope of corrupting them. Week after week he preached to a gathering in the village square and soon he had built up a large following.

All was going well with the Devil's plan until one day Robin Ruthven caught sight of the Devil's feet beneath his cloak. He was without shoes and instead of feet he had cloven hooves. When Ruthven exposed the Devil it is said that he rose above the rooftops 'like a fiery dragon' in his anger. That is why it is said to be difficult to get an Auchtermuchty person to heed a sermon.

The route begins in the car park in Orchardflat. Turn left on to Station Road and proceed to the junction with Cupar Road (A91) and carry straight on into Burnside following the Kingdom of Fife Cycle Route signs. Go along this road passing the old parish church on the left and the Cycle Tavern on the right. The name of this road changes first

## INFORMATION

**Distance:** 25 km (15.6 miles) circular route.

**Map:** OS Landranger, sheets 58 and 59; Kingdom of Fife Cycle Ways Howe of Fife West map.

**Start and finish:** Auchtermuchty—car park in Orchardflat. However, for those who would prefer to use public transport the route could just as easily begin from Ladybank Station.

**Terrain:** For all of the way this route follows sections of the Kingdom of Fife Cycle Route. After the prolonged hill during the first 5 km this route is generally very flat, with short stretches of slightly undulating road.

**Refreshments:** Available in Auchtermuchty, Ladybank, Falkland and Freuchie.

Kingdom of Fife Cycle Route
at Auchtermuchty.

to Distillery Street and then to Newburgh Road (B936). Soon open country is reached and the road begins to ascend steadily for about 3 km. At this point you come to a junction with a minor road. Here turn right and follow the green cycle sign for Ladybank and Kingskettle. Once you are on this minor road the gradient is much steeper, and after passing through a farmyard it becomes a very steep climb to the top of Weddersbie Hill, on which there is an infamous bog known as the Red Myre. So don't be too proud to dismount and walk. After about 1½ km the top of this hill is reached. This is a good opportunity to take a welcome break from the rigours of the cycling and have a look at the fine view over the Lomond Hills beyond the Howe of Fife.

Now begin the descent to the flat lands below. However, a word of warning. This is a narrow road with many twists and turns and some blind bends, so keep your speed well under control.

After passing through the tiny village of Rossie the junction of the A91 is reached. Here turn left on to this busy trunk road and, once again taking extreme care, continue along it for about 800 m. Turn right on to a minor road signposted for Charlottetown. The route is now almost completely flat all the way back to Auchtermuchty.

This flat road winds its way through a wood to a road junction at Easter Kilwhiss. Here turn left and follow the road to Charlottetown, and cross the B937 still following the cycle signs to Ladybank. At the junction of the A92, turn right and immediately left through a kissing gate and into the edge of Ladybank at Beech Avenue. Turn right into Melville Road, which then becomes Victoria Street, and follow this road to Ladybank Station.

The historic railway station at Ladybank.

Turn right into Commercial Road and then immediately left into Commercial Crescent. After going under the railway bridge, turn right into Kingskettle Road (B9129). Once at Kingskettle, turn left into Main Street and then right into South Street, with its traffic-calming measures, which then becomes Rumdewan. At the end of this street turn right under another railway bridge, after which the road turns at right angles and heads towards Freuchie. Cross the A914 and go on into Freuchie. Turn right to join High Street (B936) and follow this road out of the village and on to Newton of Falkland and then to Falkland. Turn right on to Pleasance. This is part of the A912, so take care here. This road becomes New Road, at which point there are cycle lanes to assist the cyclist. Using these, carry on a short distance to the junction of the B936 and turn right on to this road. Here the cycle lanes continue along this long, straight and flat road for almost 3 km to Dunshalt. Turn left and join the road signposted to Auchtermuchty. This road carries on for the remaining 1 km back to where the route began, passing Myres Castle on the way. This castle was built around 1530 by the Scrymgour family who, as with many of these Norman families, were originally brought to Scotland by King David I. This castle has been passed from family to family throughout the ages, and is one of the few of its type which appears to have been occupied continuously throughout its existence. It was fully restored in the 1960s.

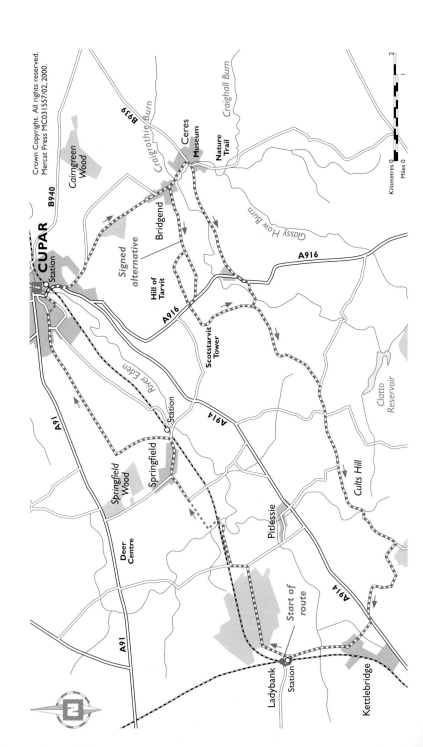

# LADYBANK TO CUPAR VIA CULTS HILL

L adybank began its life in the 1850s as a railway town, built at the point where the railway line from the Forth Bridge split to go to Perth and Cupar. This line was built on land drained during the eighteenth century and was formerly known as Our Lady's Bog. As a community developed there this name was changed to the more genteel Ladybank. The area of Monkstown in the southern quarter of the town is the only part of the settlement that predates the building of the railway. Here the monks of Lindores Abbey used to cut peat. The town was designated as a burgh in 1878 and developed a thriving linen industry.

The railway station at Ladybank is the oldest unaltered station in Scotland and therefore a place of interest in its own right.

Leave Ladybank Station at Commercial Road, immediately turn left into Commercial Crescent and carry on to a three-way junction. Here turn left, following the sign for Springfield. After 2 km another T-junction is reached. Here turn left again, still following the signs to Springfield. After a short distance, at a railway level crossing, there is a path off to the right. Take this path, but with care, as the surface is very rough in places. This path carries on for 2.8 km all the way into Springfield.

The cycle path enters Springfield at Muir Road. Turn left into Manse Road and then immediately right, and carry on along Station Road out of the village following the cycle signs to Ceres and Cupar. Here the traveller will experience the first short hill of the route. Following the cycle signs, enter Cupar at Westfield Road, then turn left into Maitland Drive, which becomes Blalowan Park with its post-world-war prefabs, and turn left into

## INFORMATION

**Distance:** 28 km (17.5 miles) circular route.

**Map:** OS Landranger, sheet 59; Kingdom of Fife Cycle Ways Howe of Fife West map.

**Start and finish:** At Ladybank Railway Station.

**Terrain:** Flat along the Howe of Fife stretch and then generally undulating, with some stretches of steep hills and rough paths in places.

**Refreshments:** Available from many places in Cupar and Ceres.

Millgate. Here, if you want to stop in Cupar, carry straight on to Crossgate and the centre of this historic town.

Cupar is a very ancient place, with evidence of a settlement here since the dark ages. Again, due to its strategic importance, there was once a castle here, although there is now no trace of it. It is said to have been constructed at the point where the Lady Burn joins the River Eden, at the end of a mound known as Moot-hill, where the Earls of Fife were alleged to have held their councils of war. It was granted a royal charter in 1381 by King Robert II and has grown in stature ever since.

Cupar was, until recently, the county town of Fife, with the offices of the local authority located there. It was also the centre of the judiciary for the county. As befitting a town of such standing it has evolved over many hundreds of years, and what is seen today reflects its development from the late eighteenth century to the present.

From Millgate, keeping to the route, turn right into South Bridge. Then turn right into South Road and follow the cycle signs for Ceres. After a short distance, take the left fork at the next junction on

The author en route to Ceres.

to the Ceres Road. The route winds uphill gradually for about a kilometre. At the top, stop and savour the beautiful 360-degree panoramic view over all parts of the Kingdom of Fife and beyond.

The road then begins to descend into Ceres. Enter Ceres on the Cupar Road, which in turn becomes Bridgend and then Main Street. At the end of this is the junction with St Andrews Road (B939). Turn right here and head out of the village continuing for almost 3 km to the junction with the A916. Turn left on to this busy road and continue for about 200 m, to where the minor road signposted to Chance Inn is located. Take this road off to the right and then descend a steep hill. At the bottom of this turn left to Chance Inn.

An alternative route is as follows. On entering Ceres at Bridgend turn right, following the cycle signs to Chance Inn and Freuchie, into Wemysshall Road. Cycle along this road for a kilometre to the entrance of Scotstarvit House. If a visit to this fine house is on the agenda, turn right and follow the estate road to the house. Scotstarvit House was built in the early part of the twentieth century by the architect Sir Robert Lorimer, in a unique combination of neo-classical and French provincial styles. The sumptuous interior is decorated in the Edwardian manner with fine collections of paintings, furniture and porcelain. The gardens too have their unique qualities, including beautiful sculpted hedges which surround the house.

After your visit to the house, continue along the estate road to where it connects with the A916. Go across this road and follow the unmade road towards the Scotstarvit Tower. Scotstarvit Tower was built between 1550 and 1579 and is an L-shaped tower house consisting of six storeys and a garret. The house is unfurnished, but is in all other respects complete and is an outstanding example of a Scottish sixteenth-century tower. Scotstarvit originally belonged to the Inglis family, but was

Scotstarvit Tower.

bought by the Scots in 1611. Sir John Scot of Scotstarvit was an eminent historian. In about 1780, the house was sold to the Gourleys of Craigrothie and then to the Wemyss family. Both the Tower and the Mansion House are owned by the National Trust for Scotland, and are open to the public between May and September. The key to the Tower is available from the Mansion House.

Once the tower has been passed, the road deteriorates greatly. In fact, it becomes a fairly difficult road to negotiate, and should only be attempted by more experienced cyclists on a mountain bike. However, having said that, this part of the route is fairly flat and only about a kilometre in length, so if it is too difficult to cycle, there is no shame in walking. This rough road emerges back on to the described route at Chance Inn.

At Chance Inn the road starts to become very hilly, going up and down quite steeply several times. The terrain changes at this point with the countryside becoming quite rugged. There are some spectacular views  over the Howe of Fife. A little further on, a fourway junction is reached. Carry straight on over here for 3 km into Coaltown of Burnturk. Here turn right, following the signs for Kingskettle. This road winds its way steeply downhill to the junction with the A92. Turn left and then, after a few metres, right on to the B9129, still signposted for Kingskettle. After 250 m or so enter Kingskettle. At the four-way junction carry straight on into Main Street and at the next junction turn right on to Ladybank Road, which is still the B9129. Follow this road into Lady-bank, turn left into Commercial Crescent and retrace the route back to the station.

Looking over the Howe of Fife.

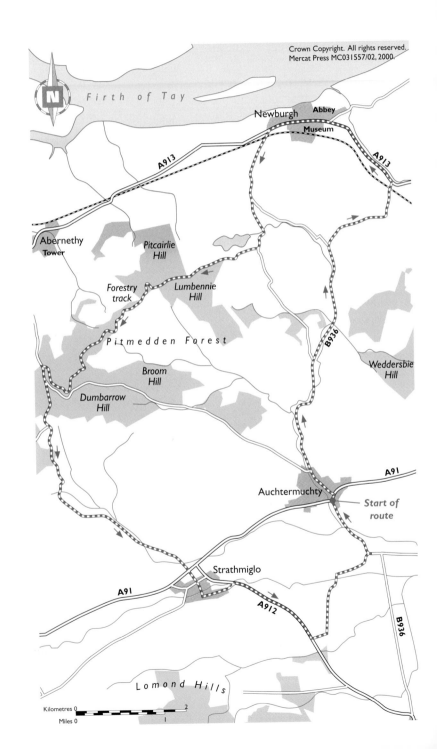

# AUCHTERMUCHTY TO NEWBURGH

The route begins in the car park in Orchardflat. Turn left on to Station Road, proceed to the junction with Cupar Road (A91) and carry straight on into Burnside following the Kingdom of Fife Cycle Route signs. Cycle along this road, the name of which changes first to Distillery Street and then to Newburgh Road (B936). Soon open country is reached and the road begins to ascend steadily for about 3 km. At this point you reach a junction with a minor road. Here continue straight on along the B936, following the cycle signs to Newburgh. After a further 2 km the cycle route splits, although both paths go to Newburgh. The route I have chosen is the one that continues straight ahead along the B936 to Den of Lindores. At the Den of Lindores turn left on to the A913, and carry on along this main road, with care, for 1½ km into Newburgh. You will pass *en route* the ruins of Denmilne Castle which was built by the Balfour family. Every part of this area has a name pertaining to Lindores. The reason for this is that the monks of Lindores Abbey extensively cultivated the entire surrounding area.

**INFORMATION**

**Distance:** 29 km (18.2 miles) circular route.

**Map:** OS Landranger, sheets 58 and 59; Kingdom of Fife Cycle Ways Howe of Fife West map.

**Start and finish:** Auchtermuchty—car park in Orchardflat.

**Terrain:** This route is generally very hilly. Follow a series of Kingdom of Fife Cycle Route signs for the entirety of this route.

**Refreshments:** Available in Auchtermuchty and Newburgh.

On entering Newburgh, turn right into Abbey Road, which is the road to Gauldry and part of the Kingdom of Fife Cycle Route. After about 200 m, on the left you will see the remains of Lindores Abbey. This scant ruin does not give an impression of the importance of this Tironensian Benedictine Abbey. It was founded in 1191 by David, Earl of Huntington, the younger brother of King Malcolm IV and William the Lion. It was one of the most celebrated and important monasteries

Travelling at pace along the Kingdom of Fife Cycle Route.

in Scotland, and because of its importance to the Roman Catholic Church it was sacked and put to the torch in 1543 by a group of zealous Protestants. The monks were expelled and the Abbey's extensive lands, cultivated for so many centuries, were confiscated.

Return to the A913, turn right and proceed through Newburgh's High Street.

Newburgh was created a burgh of barony by Alexander III. It was confirmed as a royal burgh in 1631 and developed as a port and market town for the surrounding area. During the eighteenth century the town was one of the two main ports in Fife, at that time handling flax. In the nineteenth century the town prospered as a centre for salmon fishing and the manufacture of linen, jute and linoleum.

The Laing Museum, next to the Library in St Katharine's Court, houses archaeological relics of the surrounding area, a unique collection of local and foreign antiquities and Australian artefacts. It was first opened in 1896. This collection was gifted to the town by Alexander Laing (1808–1892). Newburgh was designated a conservation area in 1969.

Finish your visit to Newburgh by going to Mugrum Pier to take in the fine views along and across the Tay before beginning the cycle trip back to Auchtermuchty. Continue along the High Street to where the War Memorial is located on the right. Here turn left into Woodriffe Road. This road climbs steadily uphill over the railway and on out of town. The incline then becomes very steep for a short distance before levelling out for a while. There is a seat by the side of the road at this point from where, whilst recovering from the exertions of the climb, there is another chance to admire the views over the River Tay, particularly where its tributary, the River Earn, joins the larger river.

Where the River Earn joins the River Tay.

Carry on to a junction. Here take the right fork and continue uphill, once again, sometimes very steeply, for about a kilometre to where a track goes off to the right. Take this rough track and begin the route through Pitmedden Forest. Soon the rough track gives way to a forest road, which although it is not tarred is not a bad surface to cycle on. This undulating route is clearly signposted and continues through forest and high hill pass for 5 km until it joins the minor road between Abernethy and Strathmiglo. Turn left on this road, and within a few hundred metres its highest point is reached next to Dumbarrow Hill. Here there is a spectacular view, almost through 360 degrees, of the surrounding countryside.

The road then proceeds downhill for 3 km and, once again, remember to take great care to keep your speed well under control, as there are quite a few tight bends; and although this is not a busy section, be careful of cars travelling in the middle of the road.

On reaching the junction of the A91, cross it and cycle along a path which joins Stocks Wynd. This leads on to High Street in the centre of Strathmiglo.

Cross High Street and continue along West Road, over the River Eden, to the junction with Cash Feus. Turn left here and carry on to the end of this road at the junction with the A912. Turn right on to the A912 and proceed along it for 2 km to the junction with the minor road signposted to Auchtermuchty. Take this road to where it joins the B936, turn left and carry on into Auchtermuchty and the end of the route.

The Cycle Tavern, Auchtermuchty—a welcome sight at the end of the route!

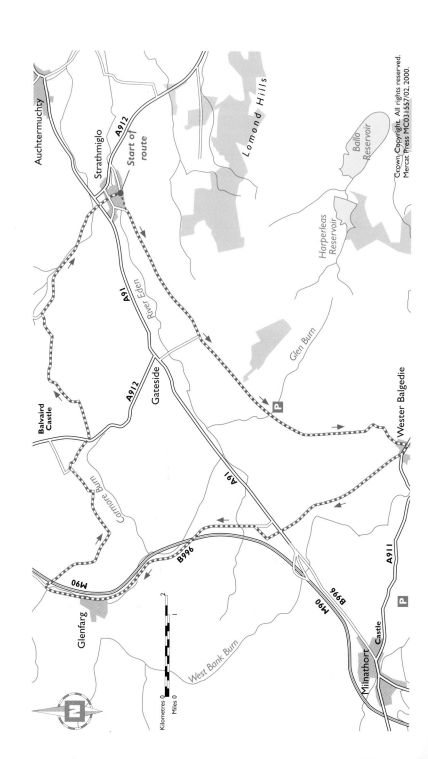

# STRATHMIGLO TO GLENFARG

Strathmiglo is an ancient burgh, once ruled by the Knights Templar, and at one time was a very important place. Its merchants supplied Falkland Palace with most of its goods and services. The dominant building of the town is the Tolbooth, with its octagonal spire and an open forestair, situated in the High Street.

Leave the High Street and turn south on to West Road and continue to the T-junction at Cash Feus. Here turn right and head along into Skene Street. At the end of this street turn left, following the Kingdom of Fife Cycle Route sign, into California, and soon open countryside is reached with West Lomond Hill towering above on the left. Carry on along this road with its very gradual incline for 3½ km to where an access path to the Lomond Hills can be found. This path is for walkers only; it is not suitable for cycles. The Lomond Hills offer many natural and historical features. One such is the Bonnet Stone, a strangely shaped sandstone rock which has been hewn by the weather over many centuries to resemble a tammy or bonnet. The base of the rock has been hollowed out to form a cave where it is said that a hermit once lived. Another piece of folklore claims that the stone covers a Pictish chieftain.

There is a legend that this area of Fife was once the centre of one of the seven divisions of the Pictish Kingdom. According to a twelfth-century Irish manuscript, Cruithne, the King of Alba, had seven sons who divided up the kingdom between them giving each division the name of a brother. The names of the seven sons were Fib, Fidach, Foltlaig, Fortrenn, Caitt, Ce and Circinn. Fib is associated with Fife, and indeed many Pictish relics have been found in this area, including a slab bearing the figure of a bull which is undoubtedly Pictish in origin.

John Knox's Pulpit is a prominent outcrop of

## INFORMATION

**Distance:** 30 km (18.7 miles) circular route.

**Map:** OS Landranger, sheet 59; Kingdom of Fife Cycle Ways Howe of Fife West map.

**Start and finish:** High Street, Strathmiglo.

**Terrain:** Flat to begin with, but generally undulating with stretches of prolonged steep climbs. Difficult.

**Refreshments:** Available in Strathmiglo and Glenfarg.

The Tolbooth, Strathmiglo.

sandstone at the top of the valley of Glenvale where, in the sixteenth century, local people who believed in the Reformation stole secretly into the hills to worship, according to their brand of Christianity, at outdoor conventicles. There are also two castles in these hills. One is Ballo Castle, a ruined manor house close to Ballo Reservoir. The other, Maiden Castle, is an ancient Bronze Age fort. These, together with many other features such as waterfalls, lochs and woodlands, make these hills an interesting place to explore on foot!

Carry on along this quiet minor road for a further 5 km. Within this stretch there is a ford and also short sections where the surface deteriorates and is sometimes quite muddy, so look out for these, and take care. Just before the end of this part of the road there is a beautiful view over Loch Leven with its many interesting islands.

At the junction with the A911, turn right and follow this road for about 200 m, then turn right at the junction at Balgedie Toll Tavern on to the B919.

At the next junction the Kingdom of Fife Cycle Route goes off to the left towards Kinross. However, we carry straight on. At the junction with the A91, cross this busy trunk road with care on to the minor road which soon joins the B996. Turn left here and go over the noisy M90 motorway which lies far below our peaceful road. Carry on along this road for 2 km into the pleasant little village of Glenfarg, where there are plenty of places to stop for refreshment. After leaving the village, continue to follow the B996 for a kilometre to a four-way junction and turn right, following the minor road signposted to Arngask. After passing over the motorway once again, climb gradually for a kilometre and take the right fork at the next junction. Continue along this road past a cemetery and on to where it turns at 90 degrees by some farm access roads. Go on again for a short distance to where the road passes through the farmyard at

Newton of Balcanquhal. Shortly after this, a T-junction is reached. Here turn left and after a little less than 100 m turn right and then follow this road downhill to the junction with the A912. On the other side of the A912 is the entrance to Balvaird Castle.

Balvaird Castle was a fifteenth-century fortified residence of a branch of the Murray family. Indeed, in 1641 Andrew Murray was created Lord of Balvaird. The Tower House is complete, whilst the surrounding court-yard is in ruins. The Tower House is open to the public during weekends in July, August and September. The property belongs to Historic Scotland.

Balvaird Castle.

Once the castle has been explored turn left out of the car park on to the A912 and continue along this sometimes busy road for a kilometre to a four-way junction, then turn right on to an unmade road and follow this onwards through a farmyard for another kilometre. When it joins with a minor road at a T-junction, turn left and follow this road uphill and through a farmyard at Leden Urquhart. Once the top of this hill has been reached there is a wonderful panoramic view over the entire Howe of Fife and beyond, so stop here and savour it for a while. The road then begins its descent towards the valley below. As with most of these minor roads there are a great number of twists and turns, so 'heed your speed'.

Soon a T-junction is reached. Turn right here and follow this road down for 2½ km to the junction with the A91. On reaching this junction, cross it and proceed along a path which joins Stocks Wynd and then goes on to the High Street in the centre of Strathmiglo.

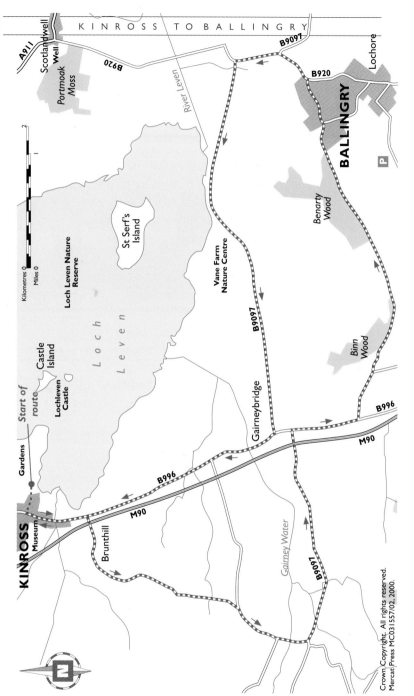

# KINROSS TO BALLINGRY VIA LOCH LEVEN

Kinross, former county town of Kinross-shire, developed in medieval times as a convenient stopping-off place *en route* between Perth and the River Forth on the Great North Road. During the eighteenth and nineteenth centuries Kinross continued as a junction and staging post on the northern coaching route and then latterly was developed as a railway junction. Alas, the railway through Kinross was closed in 1970. Today the town is noted for its cashmere-spinning industry.

Kinross is on the banks of Loch Leven, an area noted for its natural beauty and also for holding a position of great importance in Scottish history. St Serf's Priory, on the largest island on Loch Leven, St Serf's Island, was first founded by the early Celtic missionaries. It was transferred to the Augustinian order by King David I in 1150 and was a dependency of St Andrew's Priory. It was in Loch Leven Castle on another island, Castle Island, in June 1567, that Mary, Queen of Scots, was imprisoned by James Douglas, Earl of Morton, who objected to her marriage to the Earl of Bothwell earlier that year. During this imprisonment her half-brother James Stewart, Earl of Moray, coerced her into abdicating in favour of her infant son James. However, her imprisonment only lasted for ten months, until she was able to escape by boat and flee to Glasgow where her allies, led by the Hamiltons, were waiting. It was on the outskirts

**INFORMATION**

**Distance:** 26 km (16.2 miles) circular route.

**Map:** OS Landranger, sheet 59; Kingdom of Fife Cycle Ways Kingdom Route map.

**Start and finish:** At the car park in Kirkgate Park, Kinross.

**Terrain:** Fairly flat with one or two minor hills. Generally an easy route.

**Refreshments:** Available at places in Kinross and the Tea-room at Vane Farm Nature Reserve.

Mary's prison on Castle Island, Loch Leven.

of Glasgow that this small army of supporters was engaged at the Battle of Langside and routed. The Queen then fled south and crossed into England, putting herself in the hands of her cousin, Queen Elizabeth, an error of judgment that was eventually to lead to her execution on 2 February 1587. Loch Leven Castle is a square, five-storey towerhouse dating from the fourteenth century. It is open to the public in the summer months. The island is accessed by boat from Kinross, a trip which is most interesting and worthwhile.

The route begins in Kirkgate, within Kirkgate Park on the banks of Loch Leven, where there is plenty of car parking. Head along Kirkgate in a westerly direction and on to Burns Begg Street, at the end of which turn left on to High Street (B996). Continue along this street and soon you are out of the town. Once in open country, take the second road on the right following the Kingdom of Fife Cycle Route sign for Townhill and Dunfermline, and carry on underneath the motorway. From here there is a splendid view of the ranges of hills which surround the Leven Valley. Carry straight on along this road for 3 km to a junction at Ard Gairnie Farm and here take the right fork. After a kilometre, take the left fork, still following Cycle Route signs for Townhill and Dunfermline, on to the B9097. After 500 m, and a gentle downhill stretch, the Cycle Route turns to the left. However, our route turns right, keeping to the B9095. Carry on along this road for just over 2 km and cycle over the motorway to the junction with the B996. Turn right, following the signs for Kelty, and proceed along this road for a kilometre to the minor road signposted for Ballingry and turn left. The road starts to climb, gradually at first, past the ancient stone bridge (described in Route 9), and then more steeply at times over the next 5 km until it enters Ballingry at Hill Street. Continue through this former mining town to the junction with the B920. Turn left and soon open countryside is reached once again. At the next junction turn left following the signs to Scotlandwell. Follow this road for a kilometre and turn left on to the B9097 signposted for Kinross. Carry on along this road for almost 3 km until you reach Vane Farm car park. Vane Farm, on the banks of Loch Leven, is a National Nature Reserve run by the RSPB. It allows a unique opportunity to look closely at the many varieties of birds which live on this internationally important wildlife sanctuary. The loch is home to over 1,000 pairs of nesting ducks, of ten different species, as well as 40,000 water fowl of other kinds, including wild geese and swans. Among the birds you may see are Whooper Swans, Pink-footed Geese, Goldeneye, Tufted Duck, Shovelers and Wigeon. To the rear of the Farm, within the inland hills, there are many varieties of raptors, including Peregrines. The reserve also supports rare plants and insects. There are cycle parking stands provided in the car park of the Centre.

Wetlands by Loch Leven, a sanctuary for water fowl of many kinds.

After exploring the delights of Vane Farm turn back on to the B9097 and carry on for 3 km, past the imposing Benarty Hill which dominates the skyline, to the T-junction with the B996. Turn right here and follow this road for 4 km back to Kinross and the car park in Kirkgate.

Benarty Hill.

# INDEX

Abercromby, 49

Aberdour, 19, 21, 22
   Castle, 21
   Easter, 21
   Golf Course, 21

Abernethy, 99

Adam, James, 25

Adam, John, 25

Adam, Robert, 25

Adam, William, 40

Alexander I, 1, 21

Alexander II, 44

Alexander III, 33, 98

Annandale, Earl of, 7

Anstruther, 47, 51, 52, 53, 63

Anstruther, Lady, 44

Asquith, Herbert Henry, 83

Athens, 12

Auchterderran, 36

Auchterfoot, 25

Auchtermuchty, 68, 69, 81, 87, 88, 89, 97, 99
   War Memorial, 98

Auchtertool, 27, 34, 37


Bahai International Community of East Fife, 61

Balcarres, 3rd Earl of, 45

Balcarres House, 45

Balcomie Castle, 56

Balfour, Sir James, 69

Balgedie Toll Tavern, 102

Ballingry, 39, 40, 105, 106

Balliol, Edward, 59

Ballo Castle, 102

Ballo Reservoir, 102

Balmerino, 67, 68
   Abbey, 71

Balmule, Valley of, 16

Balmullo, 71, 72

Balvaird Castle, 103

Bannockburn, Battle of, 13, 63

Bass Rock, 51

Beaton, Cardinal David, 59, 69

Bell Rock Lighthouse, 57

Bellenden, Sir John, 48

Bernham, Bishop de, 73

Berwick Law, 51

Blairadam Forest, 16

Blairhall, 3

Bo'ness, 15

Bonnet Stone, 101

Bothwell, Earl of, 105

Bottomcraig, 67, 68, 71

Bower, Walter, *see* Inchcolm Abbey

Bowershall, 16

Bowhill, 36

Braefoot Bay, 21

Braid, James, 44

Breadalbane, 65

British Museum, 12

Broomhall, 12, 13

Broomhall House, 12

Broughty Ferry, 73

Brown, Thomas, *see* Pittenweem: Witch Trials

Bruce, Sir William, 76

Bruce, Sir George, 4, 12

Bryce, David, 45

Burn, William, 45

Burnturk, 30, 85, 95


Calminning Castle, 56

Campbell-Bannerman, Sir Henry, 84

Canmore, Malcolm, 1

Cardenden, 33, 36-7

Carnbee, 51

Carnegie, Andrew, 2, 7, 11

Carnock, 3

Castle Island, 105

catchpole, 79

Cellardyke, 53

Ceres, 30, 59, 61, 63, 65, 91, 92, 93

Chance Inn, 93, 95

Charles I, 2

Charles II, 25, 80

Charlestown, 11, 12

Charlottetown, 88

Clack Mannan, *see* Stone of Mannan
Clackmannan, 7, 9
Clark, Jim, 67
Cleich Mill, 17
Cleish, 16
Colinsburgh, 43, 45
Comley Park, 11, 13
Comrie, 3
Corphat, Janet, *see* Pittenweem Witch Trials
Corrie Centre, 36
Corrie, Joe, 36
Cove Wynd, 48
Cowdenbeath, 17, 34
Craigsanquhar Hotel, 72
Craigtown Country Park, 61
Crail, 47, 51, 53, 55, 57
    Museum & Heritage Centre, 56
Crawford, Earl of, 48
Cromwell, Oliver, 20
Crook of Devon, 17
Crossgates, 19, 22, 61
Cruithne, King of Alba, 101
Culross, 1, 3-4, 7, 8, 9
    Abbey, 3-4
    Bessie Bar's Hall, 3
    Coal Mine, 4
    Palace, 3, 4
    Study, 3
    Town House, 3, 4
Cults
    Hill, 30, 83, 85, 91
    Kirk, 84
Cunzie House, 53
Cupar, 45, 48, 51, 65, 67, 69, 83, 87, 91, 92, 97

Dairsie
    Castle, 61
    Kirk, 61
    Mains, 61
Dalgety Bay, 20
Damley, Lord, 41
David I, 1, 55, 59, 89, 105
David II, 7, 47
Deep Sea World, *see* North Queensferry

Defoe, Daniel, 64
Den of Lindores, 97
Denmilne Castle, 97
Dirleton, 44
Donibristle House, 20
Douglas, James, Earl of Morton, 105
Dour Burn, 21
Dumbarrow Hill, 99
Dundee, 68, 69, 71, 73
    Discovery Quay, 71
    Olympia Leisure Centre, 71
    Railway Station, 71
Dundonald, 36
Dunearn Country Woodland, 27
Dunfermline, 1, 2, 5, 9, 11, 12, 13, 15, 17, 27, 106
    Abbey, 1, 25
    Academicals Football Club, 15
    Comley Park, 2
    Pittencrieff Park, 2
    Railway Station, 1, 15
    Royal Palace, 1
    St Margaret's Park, 15
Dunshalt, 81, 89
Dysart, 25

Earlsferry, 43, 44
Earlshall Castle, 76
East Grange, 3
East Neuk, 45, 48, 52
East Shore, 53
Easter Kilwhiss, 88
Eastport, 81
Eden Valley, 79, 81
Edinburgh, 23, 25
Edward I, 1
Elgin, Charles 5th Earl of, 12
Elgin, James Bruce 8th Earl of, 12
Elgin, Thomas 7th Earl of, 12
Elgin Marbles, 12
Elie, 43, 44, 45, 47
Ermengarde, Queen, 68
Errol, Earl of, 68
Erskine, William, 8
Falkland, 79-80, 81, 83, 87, 89
    Palace, 79-80, 83, 101
    Royal Tennis Club, 79

Fall, Janet, *see* Anstruther, Lady
Feus, 72, 99
Fife Coastal Path, 19, 20, 22
Fife Ness, 55, 56
Fife Water Ski Club, 35
Fifeness Harbour, 56
Fincraigs, 68
Firth of Forth, 21, 23, 25, 34, 40, 44, 48, 51, 57, 64, 65
Forest Mill, 7
Forth Bridge (Railway), 51, 91
Forth Road Bridge, 15, 23
Freuchie, 79, 81, 83, 85, 87, 89

Gairney Water, 17
Gauldry, The, 67, 68
George III, 25
Gladstone, William, 84
Glasgow, 3, 25, 105
Glasgow Celtic Football Club, 36
Glasgow Rangers Football Club, 37
Glenfarg, 101, 102
Glenrothes, 85
Glenvale, valley of, 102
*Gododdin*, 4
Goldeneye, 107
Grainger, Thomas, 73
Grampian Mountains, 65
Grange, The, 71
Guardbridge, 75

Hallyards
    Castle, 34
    Mansion, 34
Hare Law, 73
Hawes Pier, *see* South Queensferry
Henry VIII, 79
Hill of Tarvit House, 93
HMS *Jackdaw*, 56
Howe of Fife, 81, 83, 85, 88, 91, 95, 103
Huntington, David Earl of, 97
Huntly, Earl of, 20

Inchcolm
    Abbey, 21
    Island, 21, 27
Inchmickery, 27

Industrial Revolution, 25
Inverkeithing, 19, 20, 22
    Battle of, 19
    Franciscan Friary, 19
    Mercat Cross, 19
    Railway Station, 19, 20
    Rosebery House, 19
    St Peters Parish Church, 19
    Tolbooth, 19
Isle of May, 48, 55, 57

James II, 25, 60
James III, 47, 79
James IV, 1, 60, 79
James V, 34, 79, 87

Kedlock, 72
Kellie
    Castle, 52, 76
    Law, 52
Kellie, Earl of, 52
Kelty, 15, 16, 17, 39, 41, 106
Keltybridge, 17, 41
Kemback, 61
Kennoway, 29, 31
Kentigern, *see* St Mungo
Kilconquhar, 43, 45, 47
Kilconquhar Estate, 45, 48
Kilmany, 67
Kilrenny, 53
Kincardine, Earl of, 12
Kingdom of Fife Cycle Network, 1, 59, 79, 81, 87
Kingdom of Fife Cycle Route, 63, 81
Kinghorn, 27, 33, 37
    Battle of, 33
    Castle, 33
    Railway Station, 33
Kinghorn, Earl of, 33
Kingseat, 17
Kingskettle, 83, 85, 88, 89
Kinneddar, Lord, 8
Kinross, 4, 7, 15, 16, 102, 105, 107
Kinshaldy Beach, 76, 77
Kirk o' Field, 41
Kirkcaldy, 25, 26, 27, 36
    Railway Station, 25

Kirkcaldy, Sir James, 34
Kirkgate, 106, 107
    Park, 105, 106
Kirkton of Balmerino, 68
Kirkton of Cults, 84
Knox, John, 55, 60, 101

Ladybank, 83, 84, 87, 88, 91, 95
    Railway Station, 91
Lady's Tower, The, 44
Laing, Alexander, 98
Laing, Mrs Beatrix, 49
Langside, Battle of, 106
Largo Bay, 64
Largs, Battle of, 33
Learmouth, Sir James, 56
Leslie, Andrew, 4th Earl of Rothes,
    41
Leuchars, 71, 72, 75-7
    Castle, 76
    Railway Station, 75
Liberty, 43
Limekilns, 12, 13
    Conservation Area, 13
    King's Cellar, 13
Lindores Abbey, 91, 97
Lindsay, Earl of, 48
Linktown, 25
Loch
    Fitty, 17
    Gelly, 35, 37
    Kilconquhar, 47
    Leven, 16, 105
        Castle, 41
    Ore, 39
Lochgelly, 33, 34, 35, 36
    Iron and Coal Company, 36
Lochore Castle, 40
Lochore Meadows Country Park, 39
Logie, 67, 72
    Estate, 72
Lomond Hills Hotel, 83, 85
Lookaboutye, 7
Lorimer, James, 52
Lorimer, Robert, 52
Lorimer, Sir Robert, 76, 93
Lower Largo, 63, 64

Lucklaw, 72
Lulach, King, 1
Lumsden, General Robert, 69
Lundin Links, 64
Lyon, Sir John, 33

Macbeth, 1, 33
Macduff, Thane of Fife, 79
Magus Muir, 63
Maiden Castle, 31, 102
Malcolm, Earl of Fife, 4
Malcolm III, 15
Malcolm IV, 55, 97
Markinch, 29
    Church, 29
    Railway Station, 30
Mary of Guise, 56
Mary, Queen of Scots, 12, 79, 105
Melrose, 68
Monck, General, 69
Monkstown, 91
Moray, 5th Earl of, 20
Moray, 6th Earl of, 20
Moray, Sir Andrew, 59
Morton, Patrick, 49
Mossmoran, 21
Mossmoran Natural Gas
    Liquefication Plant, 21
Motray Water, 67
Mountquhanie, 69
Mugrum Pier, 98
Murray, Andrew, Lord of Balvaird,
    103
Myres Castle, 89

Napoleon, 73
National Trust for Scotland, 3, 5, 69
Naughton House, 68
Netherlands, 4, 19
New Gilston, 65
Newburgh, 68, 69, 88, 97, 98
    Laing Museum, 98
Newmills, 5
Newport, 67, 71
Newton of Balcanquhal, 103
Nivingston Country House and
    Restaurant, 17

North Berwick, 44
North Kinneddar, 8
North Queensferry, 23
    Heritage Trust, 23
North Sea Cycle Route, 23
Northern Railway Company, 73

Oakley, 3, 5, 8, 11
Our Lady's Bog, 91
Oxford, 25

Parthenon, 12
Peat Inn, 51, 61, 63, 65
Peregrines, 107
Perth, 27, 40, 91, 105
Pictish Kingdom, 101
Pink-footed Goose, 107
Piteadie Castle, 26
Pitlessie, 84
Pitmedden Forest, 99
Pitscottie, 61
Pittenweem, 47, 48, 49
    Witch Trials, 49
Pleasance, 81, 89
Polish Paratroops, 44
Prestfield, 85
Prestonhill Quarry, 20
Puddledup, 37

Raeburn, Sir Henry, 84
Raith Rovers, 26
Rankin, Ian, 36
Ravenscraig
    Castle, 25
    Park, 25
Rebus, Inspector, see Rankin, Ian
Red Myre, 88
Reformation, 59
Richardson, Robert, 12
River
    Earn, 98
    Eden, 61, 83, 92, 99
    Forth, 5, 15, 22, 27, 105
    Tay, 68, 98
Robert I (Robert the Bruce), 7, 12,
    13, 63
Robert II, 33, 92

Robert III, 19
Rossie, 88
Rosyth, 15
RSPB, 107
Ruby Bay, 44
Ruthven, Robin, 87

Saline, 8
Saltire, 59
Scot of Scotstarvit, Sir John, 94
Scotichronicon, see Inchcolm: Abbey
Scotlandwell, 107
Scotstarvit Tower, 93
Scott, Sir Walter, 8
Scott, Sir William (of Ardross), 43
Scottish Fisheries Museum, 53
Scrymgour family, 89
Secret Bunker, 51
Seton family, 20
Sharp, James, 56
Shoveler, 107
Silversands Bay, 22
Smith, Adam, 25
Solway Moss, 79
South Queensferry, 21, 23
Springfield, 84, 91
St Abb's Head, 56
St Adrian, 55
St Andrew, 59
St Andrew's, 44, 47, 48, 49, 51, 56,
    59, 60, 61, 63, 72, 73, 75, 77, 105
    Castle, 59
    Cathedral, 59
    Cathedral Museum, 59
    University, 60
St Athernase Church, 73
St Bridget's Kirk, 20
St Columba, 29
St David's Bay, 20
St Drostan, 29
St Fillan, 48
St Fillans Church, 21
St Johnstone (Perth), 40
St Margaret (Wife of Malcolm III), 15
St Mary's on the Rock (church), 60
St Monance, 45, 47, 49
St Mungo, 3, 4

St Rule, 59
St Rule's Tower, *see* St Andrews
    Cathedral
St Salvator College, *see* St Andrews
    University
St Serf, 3-4
    Island, 105
    Priory, 105
Star, 30
Star of Markinch, 85
Stenhouse Reservoir, 27
Stevenson, Robert, 53, 57
Stevenson, Robert Louis, 53
Stewart, James (Bonnie Earl of
    Moray), 20
Stewart, James Earl of Moray (Re-
    gent), 105
Stone of Mannan, 7
Strathkinness, 60-1
Strathmiglo, 16, 83, 99, 101
Strathmore, Earl of, 33
Stuart, John Patrick, 80

Tay Bridge (Railway), 73
Tay Road Bridge, 71
Tayport, 72, 73, 75-7
Tentsmuir Forest, 73, 76
Thomson, John, 36
Torryburn, S
Town Loch, 16
Townhill, 16, 17, 106
Townhill Country Park, 16
Tufted Duck, 107

Union of the Crowns, 80
Unthank, 81

Valleyfield
    Colliery, 5
    High, 5
    Low, 5
Vane Farm, 107
Vikings, 33

War of Independence, 12, 59
Waterloo, 73

West Fife General Hospital, 16
West Lothian, 23
Wester Aberdour, 21
*Wealth of Nations, The, see* Smith,
    Adam
Whooper swans, 107
Wigeon, 107
Wilkie, Sir David, 84
William I (The Lion), 7, 33, 19, 68,
    97
William the Conqueror, 68
Williamsburgh, 43
Wishart, George, 59
Wormit, 67, 71